AF473858

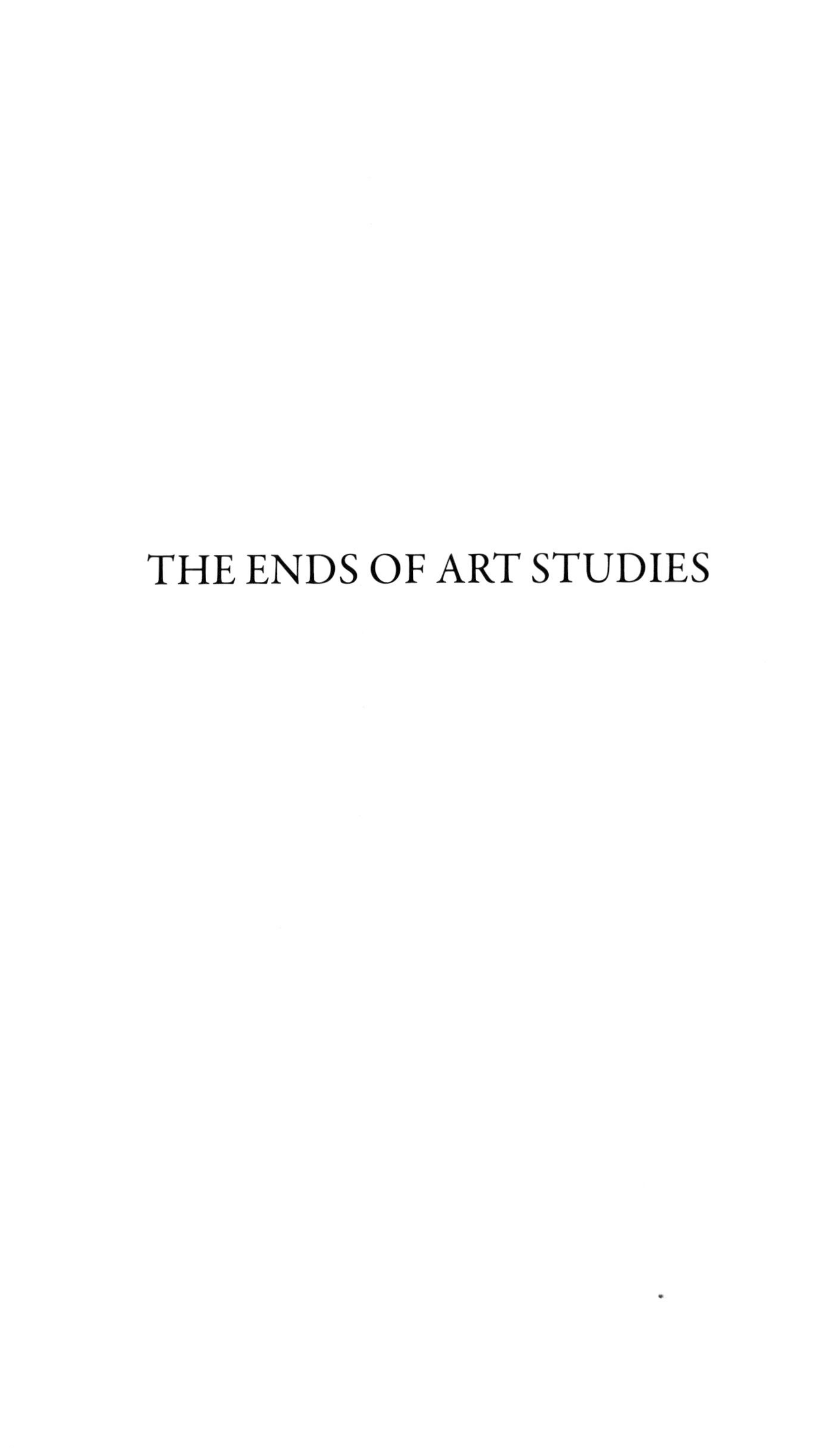

THE ENDS OF ART STUDIES

THE ENDS OF ART STUDIES

Time, Transcendence and Boundaries

FAN BAIDING

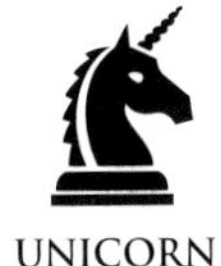

UNICORN

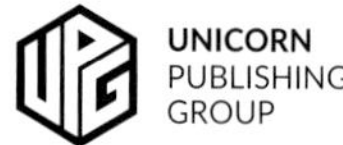

Published in association with CNPIEC by Unicorn
an imprint of Unicorn Publishing Group, 2026
Charleston Studio
Meadow Business Centre
Lewes, BN8 5RW

www.unicornpublishing.org

Cataloging-in-Publication (CIP) Data
The Ends and Borders of Kunstwissenschaft/ Fan Baiding,
Translated by Ban Haidong. – Beijing: The Commercial Press, 2024.
ISBN 978 - 7 - 100 - 23489 - 4
1. ① The... II. ① Fan... III. ① Art History – Historiography – China IV.
① J120.9
National Library of China CIP Data C-2024-052519

Translated by Ban Haidong, Shandong Technology and Business University

10 9 8 7 6 5 4 3 2 1

ISBN: 978-1-917458-07-8

Printed by Bell & Bain Ltd, Glasgow

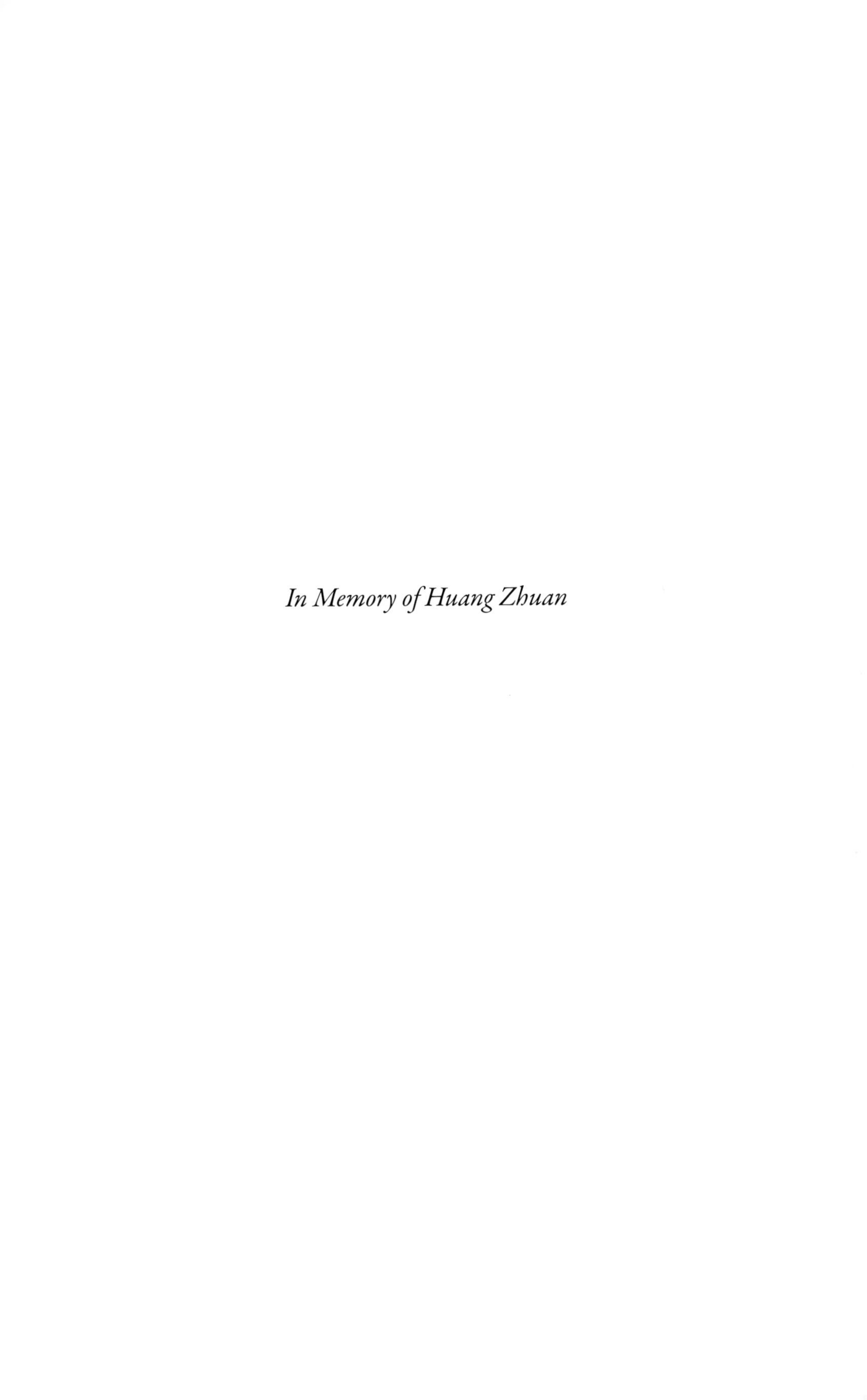

In Memory of Huang Zhuan

CONTENTS

PREFACE

Preface to the English Edition

I would like to express my sincere gratitude to Dr Joshua Gong of Unicorn Publishing Group, whose initiative and dedication made the publication of this English edition possible. I am likewise grateful to Ban Haidong for his accurate and fluent translation.

Given the book's theoretical complexity and the frequent use of specialised terms, translating it was by no means an easy task. My sincere thanks also go to Dr Paul Taylor, who not only corrected many academic and translational errors during his careful reading of the manuscript, but, more importantly, contributed valuable insights into the arguments presented in the book. I have personally proofread the entire text and made further revisions and adjustments. In the original Chinese edition, some references were cited from Chinese translations of foreign works; in this English edition, I have made every effort to replace them with the original sources or their English versions. I would like to make this point clear here.

Original Preface

My study of the intellectual growth of Erwin Panofsky (1892–1968) revealed several key questions about the development of modern art historiography. These questions are not confined to any one art historian but involve a broader community of late nineteenth-century art historians, who worked under – or identified themselves with – the banner of *Kunstwissenschaft*. Later, during my visiting research at several institutions, I collected rare literature on *Kunstwissenschaft* in China and compiled a rather clear structure for this book.

Between the mid-nineteenth and early twentieth centuries, German-speaking art historians exhibited an intense desire to establish the independence of art history, that is, to have it seen as an independent discipline. This aspiration drove them to develop distinctive methodologies, identify universal artistic principles, trace historical patterns of artistic evolution, and establish the philosophical foundations or conceptual categories specific to art studies. In essence, though their aspirations varied, they sought to give art history the scientific status enjoyed by other modern disciplines. These scholars drew upon ideas, concepts, theories, approaches and methods from other disciplines and fields to shape the academic identity of art history. However, they repeatedly emphasised the unique nature of art as their subject of study, attempting to construct a knowledge structure by clarifying research questions, methodologies, and fundamental epistemological concepts of the study of art, thereby validating art history as a discipline.

The primary questions addressed in this book arise from such a state of anxiety within *Kunstwissenschaft*. A common approach has been to analyse art history's theoretical characteristics solely from within the discipline itself. However, this approach has made it challenging to answer some questions whose origins often extend beyond the boundaries of art history. This is particularly true for *Kunstwissenschaft* at the turn of the twentieth century, which sought to challenge the barriers created by the increasing specialisation of modern academic disciplines. Without the theoretical tools from other fields, *Kunstwissenschaft* might never have developed, let alone achieved disciplinary autonomy.

It is precisely through its entanglement with the external intellectual environment that we are able to gain a clearer understanding of its overall vision and the shape of its discipline. More specifically, this book adopts three perspectives, focusing on historical development, fundamental questions and the boundaries of knowledge to illuminate the general objectives, theoretical sources, modes of reasoning and academic dilemmas that characterised art history during this period.

Chapter One begins with the perspectives on time held by *Kunstwissenschaft* scholars. Their conception of time significantly shaped the development of art history and provided an alternative way to understand their research methodologies. While numerous works address time, and some art historians have specifically written about historical time, this topic has received relatively limited attention from the perspective of art historiography theory. Previous studies in art historiography focused primarily on the ideas and methods of individual art historians, particularly their approaches to analysing specific artworks, classifying artistic styles and interpreting artistic phenomena. However, these studies rarely examine the historical frameworks within which scholars situated specific objects of study. In fact, the methodologies developed by *Kunstwissenschaft* scholars were, to some extent, linked to a shift in the understanding of time to one that differed from earlier, traditional conceptions. The changing approach to understanding historical time directly affected how they perceived and interpreted artistic phenomena. Furthermore, those who believed in the scientific nature of art research sought to establish universally applicable principles. This required that their methods remain effective beyond the constraints of time and place, transforming a previously singular, chronological narrative into more sophisticated historical models. In Chapter One, I briefly trace the possible premises behind the evolution of the conception of time within *Kunstwissenschaft*. Then, I explain how these scholars replaced abstract notions of time with a historically grounded mode of thinking that emphasised the common element of art with a tendency towards hypostatisation. Finally, I will examine the periodicity of the development in the study of art history that emerged from this new conception of time.

Chapter Two addresses the ultimate pursuit of *Kunstwissenschaft*. Whether it is the *künstlerische Probleme* ('artistic problems') discussed by Erwin Panofsky and Edgar Wind (1900–1971) or the 'structure' proposed by the Vienna School of Art History, all point toward a metaphysical realm that transcends empirical experience. It is precisely the relentless inquiry into the nature of art research that allowed *Kunstwissenschaft*, after decades of development, to reach an unparalleled high point as a theory by the early twentieth century, while simultaneously entering a period of stagnation Following Julius von Schlosser's (1866–1938) perspective, I loosely categorised art historians from Rudolf Eitelberger (1817–1885) to Hans Sedlmayr (1896–1984) into three generations, corresponding broadly to three phases of *Kunstwissenschaft*. The first generation established empirical research with an initial adoption of a scientific attitude; the second classified types of visual cognition and identified universal principles of art; the third believed in their ability and obligation to penetrate the core meaning of Art while striving to construct abstract theoretical frameworks at the epistemological level to guide art research. I describe this progression as a turn from the empirical to the transcendent. Panofsky, Wind and Sedlmayr each wrote programmatic theoretical essays that introduced new concepts and systems reflecting their visions for *Kunstwissenschaft*. Through a close and comparative reading of these three essays, we can clarify the specific reasons behind their dissatisfaction with the scholarship of preceding generations while revealing their differing views on how *Kunstwissenschaft* approached the construction of metaphysical systems.

Chapter Three explores the relationships between *Kunstwissenschaft* and other fields. Although Aby Warburg (1866–1929) was trained as an art historian, he chose to name his library after cultural science, advocating for what he termed *kunstgeschichtliche Kulturwissenschaft* and encouraging scholars to transcend disciplinary boundaries. While studying the revival of ancient culture in Renaissance Italy, he travelled as far as the Americas to visit Native American reservations, and years later, drawing on this journey, he sought to identify the 'stereotypes' that might connect classical paganism with foreign civilisations. His research perspective effectively highlighted the connections between art history and both anthropology and *Völkerpsychologie* during this period. Moreover, in their effort to establish *Kunstwissenschaft* as a scientific discipline, scholars drew widely upon findings from physiology, psychology and aesthetic formalism to address questions concerning visual perception, the relationship between body and world, and the concept of Einfülung with the animistic sense. When discussing the evolution of art, *Kunstwissenschaft* often adopted expressions from biology and evolutionary theory. One can weave a dense and intricate network of knowledge around *Kunstwissenschaft* that encourages one to view art history from a perspective of connectivity rather than isolation, thereby revealing its multidimensional academic features. Furthermore, this external-to-internal approach reveals previously overlooked thoughts underlying classical methods and concepts within the field.

Although this book centres on *Kunstwissenschaft*, I hesitate to emphasise it as a strictly defined term with fixed connotations. Instead, I hope readers will focus on its diverse and multifaceted origins and its cross-disciplinary nature. While the term remains current in art history teaching and research in German-speaking countries, I consider it, at least in this book, a product of a specific historical period. The editor of *Metzler Lexikon Kunstwissenschaft* (2011) suggests that *Kunstwissenschaft* includes both empirical and theoretical aesthetics art history – two approaches that successively served as pathways towards 'science' for nineteenth-century art history.[1] First, the philological mode of approach, if we adopt Lionello Venturi's (1885–1961) view, grounded art history on empirical evidence, effectively decomposing art into its subject, technique, style and other elements. Art historians use reliable sources to build their arguments and develop their viewpoints. However, Venturi identified a fundamental gap between this document-based art research and the essence of art itself. Too often, he argued, art historians focused on the documents rather than the art: 'The monuments of art were considered only as documents of the knowledge of the religion, the habits and customs, the characters of people, their intellectual and practical life – everything except their artistic imagination. Now without being aware of it, now with full consciousness, the philologists renounced the great conquest of the eighteenth century: the consciousness of the autonomy of art'.[2] In Venturi's view, the study of iconography, the history of technology, and the history of abstract formal elements are not, in themselves, art history. While these fields provide abundant facts about art, they lack a reflection on art itself. For this reason, Anton Springer (1825–1891) mocked Herman Grimm's (1828–1901) romantic approach as 'pop literature',while Venturi criticised Springer for lacking artistic perception.

Similarly, Michael Podro (1931–2008) identified two approaches to art history research in the nineteenth century. One focused on historical facts, requiring us 'to provide answers on diverse matters of fact, on sources, patronage, purposes, techniques, contemporaneous responses and ideals – the kind of question we can broadly describe as archaeological.' The other focused on artistic concepts, 'requiring us to see how the products of art

[1] Ulrich Pfisterer (Hrg.), *Metzler Lexikon Kunstwissenschaft: Ideen, Methoden, Begriffe*, 2, erweiterte und aktualisierte Auflage, Stuttgart, Weimar: Verlag J.B. Metzler, 2011, S. IX.

[2] Lionello Venturi, *History of Art Criticism*, trans. Charles Marriott, New York: E. P. Dutton & Co., Inc., 1964, pp. 215-216.

sustain purposes and interests which are both *irreducible* to the conditions of their emergence as well as *inextricable* from them.'[3] Podro argued that these approaches were mutually dependent and, thus, indispensable to each other: 'If a writer diminishes the sense of context in his concern for the irreducibility or autonomy of art, he moves toward formalism. If he diminishes the sense of irreducibility in order to keep a firm hand on extra-artistic facts, he runs the risk of treating art as if it were the traces or symptom of those other facts.'[4]

In Chapter One, I discuss how historical thinking entered art history research through nineteenth-century historicism. This approach prompted many scholars to trace the sociocultural conditions of artworks at specific points in time and space, yielding rich historical facts about art. However, as Jaś Elsner has observed, the German term *Kunstgeschichte* differs from the 'history of art' in French and Italian traditions. While the latter emphasises examining art within historical dimensions, the former implies not only history evidenced through art but also art explicated through history, thus concerning both history and art.[5]

The historical dimension of art history requires the discipline to extensively incorporate methods and ideas from other academic fields, thereby establishing a rigorous academic identity. Meanwhile, the artistic dimension has compelled *Kunstwissenschaft* to part ways with other disciplines, attempting to capture the essence of art beneath its physical appearance within a tailored category of knowledge. Unfortunately, *Kunstwissenschaft* came to an abrupt end in the Second World War, fading away in its final moments of brilliance and, ultimately, becoming a part of history itself.

Since then, art history has studied various research subjects and perspectives, yet it has rarely regained the intense sense of disciplinary mission that once arose from its field. At most, it has generated collective assumptions guided by various topics or theoretical frameworks, such as the recent turn towards globalisation. Most of these topics are premised on trust in the plurality of art and art history, thus placing greater emphasis on studying art within

[3] Podro, Michael, *The Critical Historians of Art*, New Haven and London: Yale University Press, 1982, p. xviii.

[4] Podro, Michael, *The Critical Historians of Art*, p. xx.

[5] Jaś Elsner, *Art History, The Global Turn and the Possibilities of Comparativism*, trans. Hu Moran (胡默然) et al., Shanghai: Shanghai People's Publishing House, 2022, p. 5, 303.

diverse historical and cultural contexts. Today, art history remains open and deliberately resists confining itself to rigid boundaries; instead, it continually dismantles its boundaries. Its limits and purposes remain unresolved and, perhaps, will continue to shift and evolve.

This book is partly based on a project supported by the National Social Science Fund of China. I have presented papers related to the theme of this book at lectures and conferences organised by Fudan University, Nanjing University, Hangzhou Normal University, OCAT Institute, and the 35th Congress of the International Committee of the History of Arts. I am grateful to Lu Mingjun, Gao Xin, Zhuge Yi, Guo Weiqi, and Anupa Pande for inviting me to participate in these events. Due to time constraints, many of the topics were not fully elaborated. I have included complete papers in this book. Chapter One, 'The Temporality and Modes of Historical Development in Kunstwissenschaft', was previously published in *Literature & Art Studies* (Issue 5, 2021). During the editing process, Zhang Ying not only corrected errors but also provided highly professional revision suggestions. When Chen Mingye shared this article on the WeChat Official account 维特鲁威美术史小组 ('Vitruvius Art History Group'), he also pointed out some oversights in the citations. When including this article in the book, I made further revisions. Bao Jingjing and Shi Guowei provided their support and assistance in publishing this book, and Dr Yu Panying meticulously compiled the bibliography. The Getty Research Institute, the Kunsthistorisches Institut in Florenz, and the Warburg Institute generously provided me with invaluable research materials and welcoming academic environments. I am particularly grateful to Paul Taylor at the Warburg Institute, who offered insightful and enlightening suggestions regarding the contents and writing. Finally, viewing this book as a progress report on my study of art history, I would like to express my sincere gratitude to Professor Fan Jingzhong and Professor Cao Yiqiang of the China Academy of Art, as well as to the many colleagues there who have guided and supported me.

I

THE TEMPORALITY AND MODES OF HISTORICAL DEVELOPMENT IN *KUNSTWISSENSCHAFT*

After nearly half a century of evolution, art history as a discipline made its achievement in methodological research in the early twentieth century. Although its claimed independence remains debatable in the interdisciplinary context of the nineteenth century, the research methods developed and the theoretical questions raised by art historians, particularly *Kunstwissenschaftlers*, established the foundations of disciplinary autonomy. These contributions have since been repeatedly cited and further developed by subsequent scholars.[1] However, among the topics about *Kunstwissenschaft*, the temporality and modes of historical development have not yet received sufficient attention. Unlike other specific concepts or methodologies that often dominate theoretical discussions, these ideas are usually embedded within *Kunstwissenschaftlers*' discourses. As one of the foundations of historical narratives of art, the temporality and modes of historical development are integral to art history, playing a significant role in its evolution into a 'science'.

It is important to note that 'temporality mode' is not a term in *Kunstwissenschaft* or art history. While Heinrich Wölfflin (1864–1945) used the term 'evolution', 'temporality', as discussed here, has a broader scope. It refers to how art historians understand time, the temporality frameworks they employ in historical narratives, and the evolutionary patterns they attribute to the development of artistic styles. By analysing the origins of

[1] While it is generally accepted that Eitelberger and his successor Moriz Thausing (1838–1884) were the first to establish art history as a discipline with *Kunstwissenschaft* as its goal, their main contribution lay in approaching artworks with a positivist attitude and scientific methods, treating them as objects of scientific investigation while rejecting the earlier aesthetic approach to art history. The term *Kunstwissenschaft* as mentioned in this chapter refers mainly to the next generation of scholars born around the 1860s, as it was their writings (published mainly in the late nineteenth and early twentieth centuries) that truly began to construct the methodological and theoretical framework of art historical research, even developing its own mode of historical development. For more on the concept of *Kunstwissenschaft* and its origins, see Regine Prange, *Die Geburt der Kunstgeschichte: Philosophische Ästhetik und empirische Wissenschaft*, Köln: Deubner Verlag für Kunst, Theorie & Praxis, 2004.

temporality in *Kunstwissenschaft*, illustrating its typical temporality mode and its relationship with contemporary thoughts of art history, I attempt to illuminate how *Kunstwissenschaftlers* constructed modes of historical development by employing the artistic commonality as their unit of time.

1. Historicism and Art History

The concept of a continuous time model in history faced increasing challenges at the turn of the nineteenth and twentieth centuries. Aby Warburg's unfinished work, *Bilderatlas Mnemosyne* (Figure 1), remains one of the most radical challenges to diachronic narratives in art history. However, he was by no means the only art historian to reflect on temporality modes; his contemporaries and predecessors had already established a tradition of engaging with questions of history and time. This tradition emerged from the crises within historiography itself, particularly those connected with the rise of historicism. This does not imply that reflections on the temporal modes of artistic development were absent before historicism; rather, studies of art history in the late nineteenth century showed distinct traces of historicism when addressing such questions. Therefore, despite the varied interpretations of the meaning of historicism[2], it is necessary to discuss certain aspects of historicism that developed alongside art history. Additionally, a brief consideration of related ideas in other disciplines will furnish a more comprehensive understanding of the potential contexts in which *Kunstwissenschaftlers* developed their consciousness of temporality.

Many have characterised the nineteenth century as the age of historiography, with Friedrich Meinecke (1862–1954), Ernst Troeltsch (1865–1923) and others acknowledging the comprehensive development of historicism in Germany.[3] After Immanuel Kant (1724–1804) and G.W.F. Hegel (1770–1831) first incorporated time as a fundamental category into philosophical systems, history and time occupied a central position in all sciences during

[2] In a widely circulated handbook on historiography, the author summarised ten manifestations of historicism, while Karl Popper's (1902–1994) conception of historicism stands as a distinct category of its own (cf. Michael Stanford, *A Companion to the Study of History*, Oxford UK & Cambridge USA: Blackwell, 1994, p. 256).

[3] Georg Iggers, *The German Conception of History: The National Tradition of Historical Thought from Herder to the Present*, Middletown, Connecticut: Wesleyan University Press, 1983, p. 5.

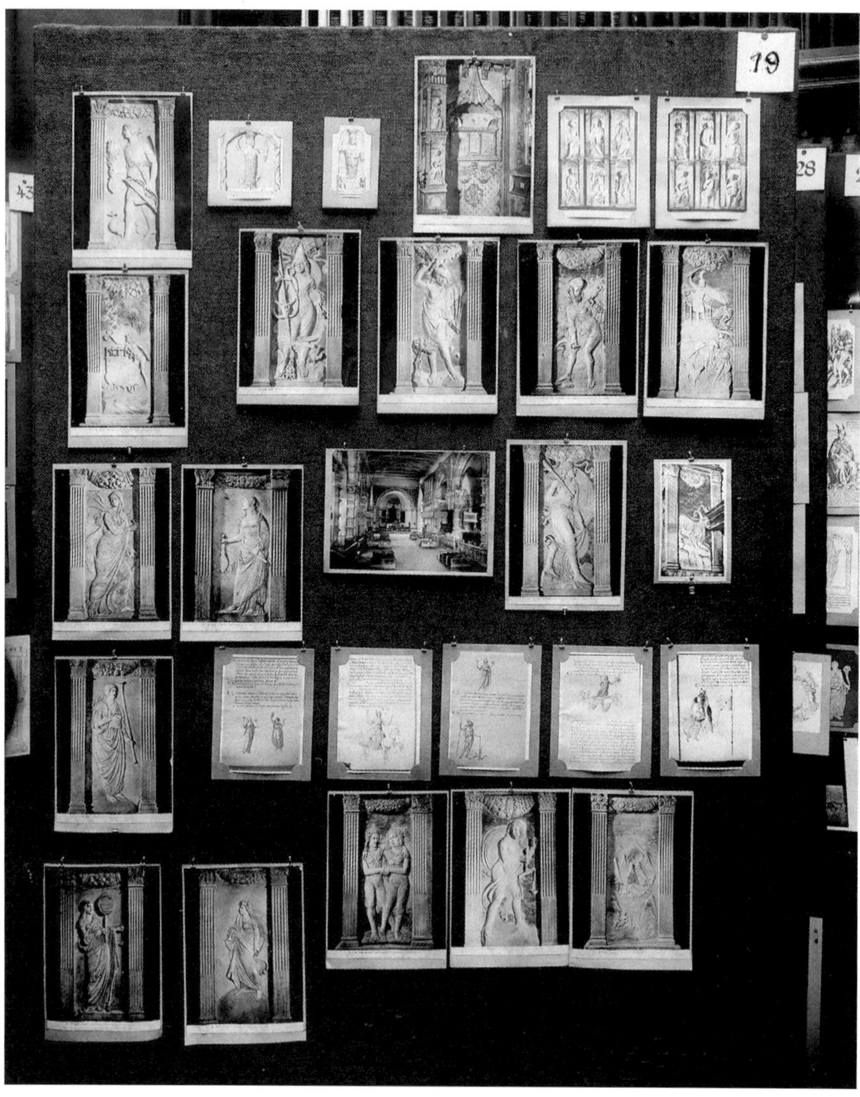

Figure 1. *Bilderatlas Mnemosyne*

the nineteenth century. Natural, cultural and artistic phenomena alike could be understood through historical approaches.[4] According to Maurice Mandelbaum's (1908–1987) definition, historicism advocates understanding and evaluating all phenomena historically; thus, phenomena must be examined within a process of development that considers their location and function.[5] But why did historical thinking become so prominent at this time? Hayden White (1928–2018) suggests that the core issue in the nineteenth-century history of ideas was defining the relationship between humanities and natural sciences, a problem that was most evident in history. Specifically, historians sought to determine whether history was an art, an empirical discipline, or even a positivist science.[6] Looking deeper, the essence of the issue was, in fact, the debate between subjectivity and objectivity, from which emerged different value judgments, methodologies, and even temporality modes in art history. Therefore, despite the varied origins and definitions of historicism, I am nevertheless willing to take the risk of discussing certain aspects that run parallel to the development of art history.

The ancient Greeks recognised the distinction between being and becoming – the former eternal, the latter changing. As Plato distinguished between knowledge and opinion, with the former representing the unchanging truths of the celestial realm, in the human world, both the things themselves and our perceptions of them are in constant in flux. Following this logic, the task of science is to discover and establish universal laws or theories that are independent of time and place. Enlightenment thinkers, relying on reason to explain the world, sought, like scientists, to uncover general laws of phenomena. They viewed humanity as a part of nature, firmly believing that human activities, like natural phenomena, adhered to unchanging laws. Historicism, however, held that truth resided in unique, specific phenomena, possessing its own temporal and spatial position in the human world, and

[4] Michael Gubser, *Time's Visible Surface: Alois Riegl and the Discourse on History and Temporality in Fin-de-Siècle Vienna*, Detroit: Wayne State University Press, 2006, p. 2.

[5] Maurice Mandelbaum, *History, Man and Reason: A Study in Nineteenth-Century Thought*, Baltimore: Johns Hopkins University Press, 1971, p. 41.

[6] Hayden White, 'On History and Historicism', in Carlo Antoni, *From History to Sociology: The Transition in German Historical Thinking*, trans. Hayden White, London: Merlin Press, 1962, p. xv.

could not be easily explained through any universal, abstract theories.[7] Georg Iggers (1926–2017) declared that historicism liberated modern thought from the two-thousand-year dominance of natural law theories, replacing that 'timeless, absolutely valid truths which correspond to the rational order throughout the universe' with an increasing appreciation for the richness and diversity of historical experience.[8] Rationalists, with their fixed standards of judgement, discerned hierarchies among phenomena, viewing the past as a lower stage in the development of reason, and, thus, inferior to the present and the future. However, early signs of historicism emerged among the Romantics, who praised the non-rationality and rediscovered value in previously dismissed historical periods.[9] Johann Gottfried Herder (1744–1803), for instance, rejected measuring cultures against any standard of superiority. Consequently, historicism established a position of relativism in both knowledge and ethics, thereby helping *Kunstwissenschaftlers* to dismantle value barriers among artworks and providing essential premises for seeking new modes of artistic development. During his student years, Alois Riegl (1858–1905) exhibited faith in historicism, while Heinrich Wölfflin, in the preface to the sixth edition of *Kunstgeschichtliche Grundbegriffe* (Figure 2), stated explicitly that his aim was not to make value judgements but to characterize styles, believing that visual types or perceptual visualization varied across time and place.[10]

Another factor contributing to this premise was Hegelianism. Hegelianism viewed history as a combination of empirical facts and ideas, representing the development of spirit in time, just as nature represented the development of ideas in space.[11] Thus, history was no longer merely an accumulation of events and dates but a phenomenon that could be interpreted within a theoretical framework. Its development was not only governed by a simple chronological order but also possessed an internal logic. E. H. Gombrich (1909–2001), in

[7] Michael Stanford, *A Companion to the Study of History*, p. 251.

[8] Georg Iggers, *The German Conception of History*, p. 5.

[9] Hayden White, 'On History and Historicism', p. xvi.

[10] Margaret Olin, *Forms of Representation in Alois Riegl's Theory of Art*, Pennsylvania: The Pennsylvania State University Press, 1992, p. 4; Heinrich Wölfflin, *Principles of Art History: The Problem of the Development of Style in Early Modern Art*, trans. Jonathan Blower, Los Angeles: The Getty Research Institute, 2015, p. 78.

[11] Ernst Cassirer, *The Myth of the State*, New Haven and London: Yale University Press, 1946, p. 255.

KUNSTGESCHICHTLICHE GRUNDBEGRIFFE

DAS PROBLEM DER STILENTWICKLUNG IN DER NEUEREN KUNST

VON

HEINRICH WÖLFFLIN

SECHSTE AUFLAGE

HUGO BRUCKMANN / VERLAG / MÜNCHEN 1923

Vorwort

Das Buch, das 1915 in erster Ausgabe erschien, wird hier zum sechstenmal in unveränderter Gestalt aufgelegt. An Stelle der langen Vorreden der früheren Ausgaben sollen aber nur wenige Sätze treten. Das, was den alten Text erklärend und erweiternd begleiten müßte, ist allmählich zu einem Umfang angewachsen, daß es nur in einem selbständigen zweiten Band untergebracht werden kann.

Zur allgemeinen Orientierung diene folgendes. Die „Grundbegriffe" sind hervorgegangen aus dem Bedürfnis, der kunsthistorischen Charakteristik eine festere Basis zu geben; nicht dem Werturteil — davon ist hier gar nicht die Rede —, sondern der Stilcharakteristik. Diese hat das größte Interesse, zunächst einmal die Form der Vorstellungsbildung zu kennen, der sie im einzelnen Fall gegenübersteht. (Man spricht besser von Vorstellungsformen als von Sehformen.) Selbstverständlich ist die Form der anschaulichen Vorstellung nicht etwas Äußerliches, sondern von bestimmender Wichtigkeit auch für den Inhalt der Vorstellung, und insofern ist die Geschichte dieser Anschauungsbegriffe bereits auch Geistesgeschichte.

Die Art des Sehens oder sagen wir also des anschaulichen Vorstellens ist nicht von Anfang an und überall dieselbe, sondern hat wie alles Lebendige ihre Entwicklung. Es gibt Stufen der Vorstellung, mit denen der Kunsthistoriker zu rechnen hat. Wir kennen altertümlich-„unreife" Sehweisen, wie wir andrerseits von „hohen" und „späten" Kunstperioden sprechen. Die archaische griechische Kunst oder der Stil der alten Portalskulpturen von Chartres darf nicht so interpretiert werden, als ob die Dinge heute gemacht worden wären. Anstatt zu fragen: „Wie wirken diese Kunstwerke auf mich (den modernen Menschen)?", und danach den Ausdrucksgehalt zu bestimmen, muß der Historiker sich vergegenwärtigen, welche Auswahl von Formmöglichkeiten die Zeit überhaupt hatte. Das wird dann zu einer wesentlich andern Interpretation führen.

Die Entwicklungslinie des anschaulichen Vorstellens ist, um einen Ausdruck von Leibniz zu gebrauchen, „virtuell" gegeben, in der Tatsächlichkeit der gelebten Geschichte aber erfährt sie die mannigfaltigsten Brechungen, Hemmungen, Umbildungen. Das vorliegende Buch will nun nicht einen Auszug aus der Geschichte bieten, sondern versucht lediglich Maßstäbe aufzustellen, an denen man die geschichtlichen Wandlungen (und die nationalen Typen) genauer bestimmen kann.

IX

VORWORT

Dabei entspricht unsere Formulierung der Begriffe nur der Entwicklung in der neueren Zeit. Für andere Perioden müssen sie immer wieder neu modifiziert werden. Doch hat das Schema sich bis in die Gebiete der japanischen und der altnordischen Kunst hinein als brauchbar erwiesen.

Der Einwand, daß durch die Annahme einer „gesetzmäßigen" Entwicklung des Vorstellens die Bedeutung der künstlerischen Individualität aufgehoben werde, ist ein läppischer Einwand. So gut der Körper nach durchgehenden Gesetzen gebaut ist, ohne daß der individuellen Form Abbruch geschähe, so gut steht die Gesetzlichkeit der geistigen Struktur des Menschen mit Freiheit nicht im Widerspruch. Und wenn man sagt, man habe wohl immer so gesehen, wie man sehen wollte, so ist das eine Selbstverständlichkeit. Es handelt sich nur darum, wie weit dieses Wollen des Menschen einer gewissen Notwendigkeit untersteht, eine Frage, die allerdings über das Künstlerische hinaus in den Gesamtkomplex geschichtlichen Lebens, ja schließlich ins Metaphysische hineinführt.

Ein weiteres Problem, das in dieser Schrift nur angedeutet, nicht durchgeführt ist, ist das Problem der Periodizität und der Kontinuität. Es ist sicher, daß man nie auf den gleichen Punkt in der Geschichte zurückkommt, aber es ist ebenso sicher, daß innerhalb der Gesamtentwicklung einzelne, in sich geschlossene Entwicklungen sich unterscheiden lassen und daß die Entwicklungslinie in diesen Perioden eine gewisse Parallelität aufweist. Bei unserer Fragestellung, wo nur der Stilablauf in der neueren Zeit analysiert wird, spielt das Problem der Periodizität keine Rolle, aber das Problem ist wichtig, freilich wird auch es vom bloß kunstgeschichtlichen Standpunkt aus nicht behandelt werden können.

Auch dieses Verhältnis: wieviel jeweilen von alten Sehresultaten in eine neue Stilperiode hinübergenommen worden ist, wie eine Dauerentwicklung sich mengt mit Sonderentwicklungen, muß erst durch Einzeluntersuchungen aufgeklärt werden. Man kommt dabei auf Einheiten ganz verschiedenen Grades. Die Architektur der Gotik kann als Einheit genommen werden, es kann aber auch die Gesamtheit der nordisch-mittelalterlichen Stilentwicklung die Einheit darstellen, deren Entwicklungskurve man herauspräpariert, und die Resultate können gleichmäßige Geltung beanspruchen. Schließlich ist auch die Entwicklung nicht immer eine gleichzeitige in den verschiedenen Künsten: neue Primitivvorstellungen in Malerei oder Plastik können z. B. eine ganze Weile mit einem weiterlebenden Spätstil von Architektur sich vertragen — man denke an das venezianische Quattrocento —, bis endlich alles auf den gleichen optischen Nenner gebracht wird.

X

VORWORT

Und wie die großen Zeitquerschnitte kein ganz einheitliches Bild ergeben, weil eben die optische Grundstimmung von Natur aus eine verschiedene ist bei den verschiedenen Rassen, so wird man auch mit der Tatsache sich abfinden müssen, daß beim gleichen Volke — ethnographisch gebunden oder nicht — verschiedene Vorstellungstypen dauernd nebeneinander vorkommen. In Italien schon gibt es diese Zwiespältigkeit, am offenbarsten aber tritt sie in Deutschland zutage. Grünewald ist ein anderer Vorstellungstypus als Dürer, obwohl beides Zeitgenossen sind. Aber man darf nicht sagen, damit sei die Bedeutung der (zeitlichen) Entwicklung aufgehoben: für den Anblick aus größerer Weite einigen sich diese zwei Typen doch wieder zu einem gemeinsamen Stil, d. h. man erkennt unmittelbar das, was eben beide als Vertreter ihrer Generation verbindet. Und eben dieses Gemeinsame bei größter individueller Verschiedenheit soll hier begrifflich gefaßt werden.

Auch die originellste Begabung kann nicht über gewisse Grenzen hinauskommen, die ihr durch das Datum der Geburt gesetzt sind. Es ist nicht alles zu allen Zeiten möglich und gewisse Gedanken können erst auf gewissen Stufen der Entwicklung gedacht werden.

München, im Herbst 1922.

H. W.

Figure 2. Preface to the sixth edition of *Kunstgeschichtliche Grundbegriffe*

his well-known essay, argued that the then-'crumbled' Hegelianism was not only the foundation of cultural history, but it also brought fundamental changes to art history. He first noted that Hegel saw the development of art as 'a logical process accompanying and reflecting the unfolding of spirit', then he stated that this logic confirmed a previous intuition that 'each art and each culture existed in its own right and could not be judged by other standards'.[12] The art history once constructed on absolute aesthetic standards had now disintegrated, enabling a new generation of art historians to reshape their own reasonable logic. From this perspective, Hegelianism contributed to the emergence of *Kunstwissenschaft*'s distinct temporality modes in at least two ways: first, it undermined chronological historical narrative modes; secondly, it infused history and art history with philosophical frameworks, thereby constructing more complex and profound temporality modes and creating opportunities for the emergence of other logics of historical development.

Hegel's concept of the 'Zeitgeist' aligns in certain ways with historicism. First, many historicists tended to combine their historicism with a form of traditional idealism derived from Kant and Hegel. In their view, history belonged to the realm of spirit, as it was composed of human thoughts, purposes, motivations and actions. Therefore, genuine historical research involved reconstructing these 'spiritual' factors.[13] With the rise of psychology in the nineteenth century, the history of spirit has developed into that field. Several key figures in the *Kunstwissenschaft* simultaneously turned their attention to psychological issues within art history, though these endeavours can still be traced back to Hegel. Moreover, Hegel maintained that philosophy was the expression of its age in thought; that is, that philosophy and other cultural phenomena were conditioned by their era. Wilhelm Dilthey (1833–1911), a prominent advocate of *Geistesgeschichte*, expressed a similar idea: 'Every world-view is historically conditioned and therefore limited

[12] E. H. Gombrich, 'In Search of Cultural History', in *Ideals and Idols: Essays on Values in History and in Art*, Oxford: Phaidon Press, 1979, pp. 28, 34.

[13] Hans Meyerhoff (ed.), *The Philosophy of History in Our Time*, Garden City, New York: Doubleday Anchor Books, 1959, p. 36.

and relative.'[14] Consequently, each era came to be associated with specific worldviews, and its distinction from the past and future was no longer measured by a mere chronological sequence, but was gradually replaced by cultural markers. These cultural signs later became the fundamental units through which art historians shaped their models of temporality.

Starting with Kant and moving through the influences of Johann Herbart (1776–1841), Gustav Fechner (1801–1887), Hermann von Helmholtz (1821–1894), Robert Zimmermann (1824–1898), Wilhelm Wundt (1832–1920), and Robert Vischer (1847–1933) (Figure 3) in psychology, physiology and aesthetics, the visual cognition of the viewing subject gradually became a focus of *Kunstwissenschaft*.[15] Visual perception and understanding varied across time and place, and spatial conceptions were not static. Thus, Alois Riegl and Heinrich Wölfflin attributed different types of spatial representation to distinct worldviews. Correspondingly, the process of artistic evolution was reinterpreted as a typology of subjective cognitive modes unfolding along a temporal trajectory. In essence, Kant shifted *Kunstwissenschaft* from an objective focus toward a subjective one.

Another significant aspect came from the insights that Charles Darwin (1809–1882), or Darwinism, brought to historical research. Although the metaphor of biological growth had long existed in human historical narratives, the popularity of evolutionary theory in the nineteenth century provided a set of natural evolutionary laws and suggested dynamic, developing, and active modes of historical development. Here, we once again observe the emphasis of historicism on becoming rather than being as its logical foundation, and its tendency to interpret reality from a relative and historical perspective. This mode of thinking, advocating for change, would ultimately lead to a crisis of values. As Hayden White states, 'Man was cast out upon a sea of flux, at the mercy of a mythological conception called time, reduced to the

[14] Wilhelm Dilthey, 'The Dream', in William Kluback, *Wilhelm Dilthey's Philosophy of History*, New York: Columbia University Press, 1955, p. 106. 'Jede Weltanschauung ist historisch bedingt, sonach begrenzt, relative', Wilhelm Dilthey, 'Traum', in Gesammelte Schriften, Stuttgart: B. G. Teubner Verlagsgesellschaft, 1961, Bd. VIII, S.224.

[15] cf. Harry Francis Mallgrave and Eleftherios Ikonomou (eds), *Empathy, Form and Space: Problems in German Aesthetics 1873-1893*, Santa Monica: Getty Center for the History of Art and the Humanities, 1994, pp. 1–85.

status of servant to values which were shown to be mere ideologies.'[16] Both Karl Popper (1902–1994) and E. H. Gombrich strongly opposed ideas that overlooked individual factors in favour of collective spirit. Nevertheless, this way of thinking was precisely one of the beginnings of *Kunstwissenschaft*.

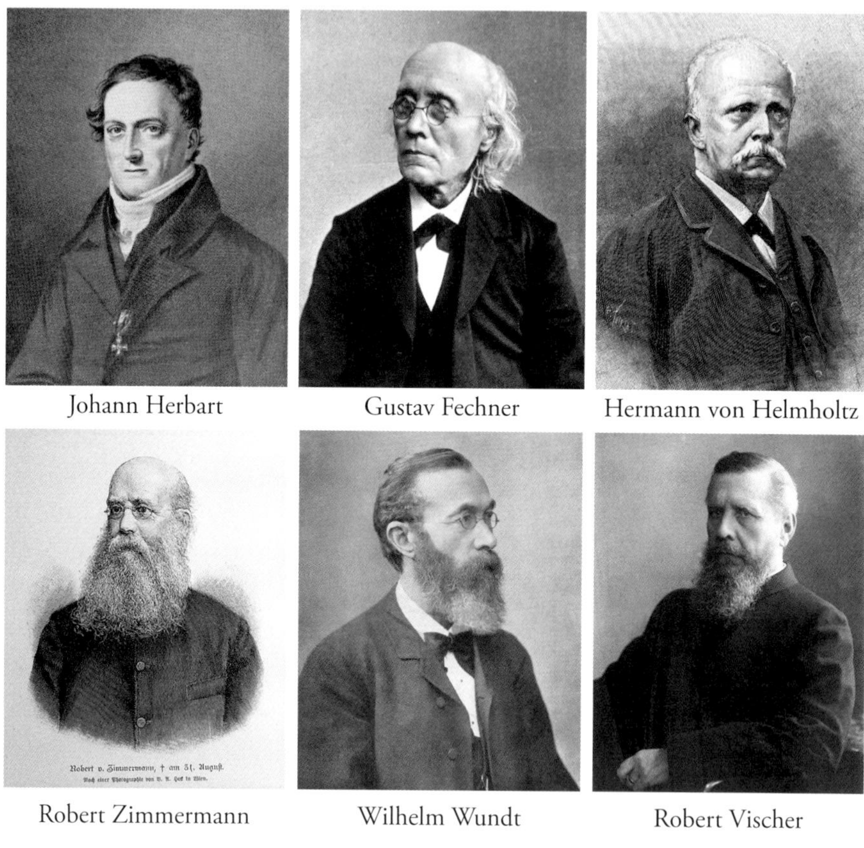

Johann Herbart | Gustav Fechner | Hermann von Helmholtz

Robert Zimmermann | Wilhelm Wundt | Robert Vischer

Figure 3.

2. Commonality as Unit of Time

Some believe that the humanities, like natural sciences, operate under universal laws, and that there is little difference between humans across time and space. David Hume (1711–1776) stated,

[16] Hayden White, 'On History and Historicism', p. xvii.

> It is universally acknowledged, that there is a great uniformity among the actions of men, in all nations and ages, and that human nature remains still the same.... Would you know the sentiments, inclinations, and course of life of the Greeks and Romans? Study well the temper and behaviors of the French and English.... Mankind are so much the same, in all times and places, that history informs us of nothing new or strange in this particular.[17]

Historicists opposed this view, arguing that people from different eras and places lived under various social systems, customs and cultures, and that this led inevitably to different ways of thinking, habits and values. However, while those historicists emphasised human differences, they referred not to individuals but to groups of people. Herder believed the determining factor in history was human – not individuals in the ordinary sense but specific groups.[18] Here, we can observe two fundamental premises that later became pervasive in art historical research: categorising art history by time and place (such as styles and modes of visual cognition); and connecting these phenomena to their environments – not deterministically but as influential factors. It was under these premises that *Kunstwissenschaftlers* could experiment with modes of artistic development that transcended both the individual and linear time.

The shift from the individual to the group is a significant characteristic that distinguished *Kunstwissenschaft* from traditional art history and served as a prerequisite for constructing its own logic of historical development. Borrowing from the title of Carlo Antoni's (1896–1959) work *Dallo storicismo alla sociologia*, this transformation essentially represented a shift from history to sociology[19] or, more precisely, from an art history focused on individual events to an art-science exploring general laws. A convincing

[17] David Hume, *An Enquiry Concerning Human Understanding*, Oxford: Oxford University Press, 2007, p. 60.

[18] However, in Herder's view, this distinctiveness originated from the inherited psychological characteristics of different races. Although he acknowledged the influence of external environment on humans, he insisted that the key to these differences lay in people's characteristics (cf. R.G. Collingwood, *The Idea of History,* Oxford: Clarendon Press, 1946, pp. 89–93.)

[19] Carlo Antoni, *Dallo storicismo alla sociologia*, Firenze: Sansoni, 1940.

contemporary figure provided evidence for this shift. In a letter to Adolph Goldschmidt (1863–1944) written in 1903 (Figure 4), Aby Warburg divided the current art historical research trends into two groups: 'I. Panegyric art history starting from the individual work of art or artist; II. History of style, starting from the restricting conditions of the typical form-giving (social) forces.' He described the second school as 'the science of typical forms ... has made its aim to investigate the sociological conditions, the universally existing inhibitions...'[20]

Having moved beyond heroic individual narratives, art historians began to create a history of art itself. They did not ignore individual artists but, rather, recognised that 'one cannot say that this nullifies the significance of the (temporal) development: the two types are reunified into one common style when viewed from a greater distance; that is, one immediately recognizes the element that binds them together as representatives of their generation.' They aimed to distill this commonality, which coexists with the most pronounced individual differences, into abstract fundamental concepts.[21] Discussions of artistic development were built upon such commonalities – universal constraints defined by specific temporal and spatial coordinates. Artistic phenomena occurring at these intersections of time and space were inevitably subject to such constraints.

What Wölfflin sought to demonstrate was a 'lückenlose Reihe' ('unbroken succession')[22] from one common element to another. His temporality model was no longer an accumulation of events presented in chronological order but, rather, an order of development composed of multiple commonalities. Consequently, the process of evolution from one common element to the next became the most intriguing transitional period – comparable to the pivotal moments of the next dynasty in chronicles. However, these two units of time correspond to two distinct conceptions of historical time. It

[20] E. H. Gombrich, *Aby Warburg: An Intellectual Biography*, Oxford: Phaidon, 1986, pp. 141–4. The complete version of this letter, titled '*Die Richtungen der Kunstgeschichte. An Adolph Goldschmidt*' is included in Aby Warburg, *Werke in einem Band*, Berlin: Suhrkamp Verlage, 2010, S. 672–9.

[21] Heinrich Wölfflin, *Principles of Art History*, p. 80.

[22] Heinrich Wölfflin, *Kunstgeschichtliche Grundbegriffe: das Problem der Stilentwicklung in der neueren Kunst*, München: F. Bruckmann A.-G., 1915, S. V.

RESULTS AND RETREAT 141

There exists a revealing draft of a letter of August 1903 in which Warburg sums up a conversation he had had with his friend, the great mediaevalist Adolph Goldschmidt. In it he presents in tabular form the whole map of the discipline of art history as he saw it. Though the letter was certainly not meant entirely seriously and was not, of course, intended for publication, it is important both for its indication of Warburg's strong dislikes and for the position he claims for himself on the map:

My dear Adolph,

The subject of our conversations on the *Lehrter Bahnhof* persisted in preoccupying me and so I assume the boldness of the ignorant (which is generally served up euphemistically as the naïveté of the innocent child), and I am writing what has come to my mind. The various trends of modern art history are derived from diverse trends which do not necessarily and organically belong together.

I

A 1. The starting points in the 15th century: the *mirabilia* literature with its natural tendency to stress and exaggerate local sights …

A 2. Panegyric hero-worship: *uomini famosi* (Petrarch *trionfi*), famous men, Castagno, the inventors of things, later Polydore Vergil, final derivation: *catalogo delle varie cose*; encyclopedia.
While this group A represents the history of art for the layman who is to experience uplift, there now arrives under B a history of art written by artists (Typical: Vasari).

B. The history of artists written from the point of view of the progressive artistic genius who increasingly conquers the technique of creating illusions up

Mein lieber Adolph,

Das Thema vom Lehrter Bahnhof hat nicht aufhören wollen, mich zu beschäftigen und so habe ich denn die Courage der Ignoranz (die man euphemistisch als Unbefangenheit des reinen Toren zu servieren pflegt) und schreibe Dir, was mir eingefallen ist. Die Richtungen der modernen Kunstwissenschaft kommen aus verschiedenen organisch nicht selbstverständlich zusammenhängenden Richtungen:

I

A 1. Ausgangspunkte im XV. S.: die *mirabilia* Literatur mit der natürlichen Tendenz, das lokal Sehenswürdige übertreibend hervorzuheben …

A 2. Die panegyrische Heroenverehrung: *uomini famosi* (Petrarcha *trionfi*), berühmte Männer, Castagno, die Erfinder der Dinge (später Polidoro Vergilio), Ausläufer: catalogo delle varie cose; Konversationslexikon.
Während Gruppe A die Kunstgeschichte, geschrieben für den Laienzuschauer, der 'erhoben' werden soll, bezeichnet, kommt unter B die Kunstgeschichte hinzu, geschrieben vom Künstler (Vasari als Typus).

B. Künstlergeschichte vom Standpunkt des fortschreitenden künst-

Figure 4. A letter written by Aby Warburg in 1903, transcribed and translated by Gombrich, in *Aby Warburg: An Intellectual Biography*

was because the historical narrative of *Kunstwissenschaft* had, intentionally or unintentionally, adopted commonality as its unit of time that scholars like Franz Wickhoff (1853–1909) and Alois Riegl could reinterpret artworks previously considered as works of declining periods. They argued that art history should highlight the value of art over time, rather than some timeless, idealised standard of perfection.

In *Die Wiener Genesis* (1895), Wickhoff distinguished three modes of visual narration: complementary, isolating, and continuous.[23] He explicitly associated each narrative mode with specific periods and locations, fixing their positions within historical coordinates. In his view, these three narrative types formed part of a continuous sequence, challenging the earlier view that the development of sculpture and painting had stagnated or ceased by the Roman period. He reinforced his argument by quoting his colleague Riegl's statement from *Stilfragen* (1893) two years earlier: 'The ancient art of the Roman Empire developed and indeed progressed upward, rather than merely declining as the widespread belief.'[24] Wickhoff reasoned that the emergence of new architectural styles in the Roman Empire made it unlikely that artistic development would have come to a halt.[25] Wickhoff's distinction between narrative types demonstrates his acute awareness of temporality in visual representation, which, as he described it, involved 'the treatment of time'.[26] Furthermore, his inference of developments in plastic arts from architectural progress indicates his assumption of the unity of cultural phenomena within the constraints of time and place. Based on these two insights, he attributed specific modes of visual narration to the products of particular *Zeitgeists*.

[23] Wilhelm Ritter von Hartel und Franz Wickhoff, *Die Wiener Genesis*, Wien: F. Tempsky, 1895, S. 6–10. The work was originally published as a supplement to volumes 15 and 16 of the *Jahrbuch der Kunsthistorischen Sammlungen des Allerhöchsten Kaiserhauses* (1895). In 1900, the introductory section written by Wickhoff was separately published in English as *Roman Art: Some of Its Principles and Their Application to Early Christian Painting*, trans. Mrs S. Arthur Strong, London: W. Heinemann; New York: Macmillan, 1900. After Wickhoff's death, the German edition, *Römische Kunst*, Berlin: Meyer & Jessen, 1912, with an introduction by his student Max Dvořák (1874–1921), was published, with minor omissions in certain passages.

[24] Alois Riegl, *Stilfragen: Grundlegungen zu einer Geschichte der Ornamentik*, Berlin: George Siemens, 1893, S. 272; Wilhelm Ritter von Hartel und Franz Wickhoff, *Die Wiener Genesis*, S. 10. Franz Wickhoff, Roman Art, p. 113.

[25] Wilhelm Ritter von Hartel und Franz Wickhoff, *Die Wiener Genesis*, S. 10.

[26] *Ibid.*, S. 60.

Riegl's theory of *Kunstwollen* ('artistic volition') also represents a universality constrained by time and space, reflecting the universal artistic impulse of humanity across different eras and cultures. In his view, there existed *Kunstwollens* of classical art, of the Roman Empire or early Christian art, and it was the changes in the artistic volition that drove the development of art.[27] He stated that:

> All such human *Wollen* is directed towards self-satisfaction in relation to the surrounding environment (in the widest sense of the word, as it relates to the human being externally and internally).... man wants to interpret the world as it can most easily be done in accordance with his inner drive (which may change with nation, location and time). The character of this *Wollen* is always determined by what may be termed the conception of the world at a given time [*Weltanschauung*] (again in the widest sense of the term)...[28]

At this point, without further examples, we should understand Warburg's classification of two prevailing trends in contemporary art historical research as the theoretical premise of the "Gourp II" scholars, who constructed modes of art history's development based on common elements of art.

3. The Reification of Time

Commonality not only became the basic unit for constructing narratives in art history but also influenced how *Kunstwissenschaftlers* perceived historical time. To further illustrate this point, we'd better first discuss two long-standing views of time. Stephen Hawking (1942–2018) wrote that 'Both Aristotle and Newton believed in absolute time. That is, they believed one could unambiguously measure the interval between two events, and that this

[27] Rolf Winkes, 'Foreword', in Alois Riegl, *Late Roman Art Industry*, trans. Rolf Winkes, Roma: Giorgio Bretschneider Editore, 1985, p. XIX. Even in the final stage of his academic career, Riegl maintained his belief that Kunstwollen depended on the worldviews of different periods. This point is discussed in the editor's prefaces of both the German and English editions of *Historical Grammar of the Visual Arts*. See Alois Riegl, *Historische Grammatik der bildenden Künste*, Graz and Köln: Böhlau Verlag, 1966; Alois Riegl, *Historical Grammar of the Visual Arts*, trans. Jacqueline E. Jung, New York: Zone Books, 2004.

[28] Alois Riegl, *Late Roman Art Industry*, p. 231.

time would be the same whoever measured it, provided they used a good clock. Time was completely separate from and independent of space.'[29] There has long been an opposing view to this, Augustine, as one of the representatives, stated that: 'I affirm myself to know thus much; that if nothing were passing, there would be no past time: and if nothing were coming, there should be no time to come: and if nothing were, there should now be no present time.'[30] For Aristotle or Newton, time was like a metal box: whether it contained anything or not, the box itself existed. Whereas, for Augustine, time was more like a balloon: it could expand or contract, exist or vanish, depending entirely on the matter within it.[31] The former conception essentially shaped the popular understanding of time. As Newton stated, absolute time 'of itself, and from its own nature flows equably without regard to anything external'.[32] Historical narratives based on chronological order were founded on this principle, but late nineteenth-century art historical writing more often reflected the latter view of time. Augustine wrote that he measured time in his mind, because events left impressions on the mind; thus, when events ended and only impressions remained, he was actually measuring impressions when measuring time. Thus, 'either therefore times do exist, or I do not measure times'.[33] Events that occur in time, like the matter that fills a balloon, become the *content* of time, transforming time into a concrete reification with a specific form. This way of thinking about time as reification is evident in the works of many *Kunstwissenschaftlers*. Erwin Panofsky stated explicitly that art historians instinctively regarded historical time as different from astronomical time. When historians mentioned a specific year, they referred to concrete events and specific cultural characteristics. In other words, they conceived time through a unit of meaning. Art historians conceived it through a unity of style.[34]

[29] Stephen Hawking, *A Brief History of Time,* New York: Bantam Books, 1988, p. 18.

[30] Augustine, *Confessions*, trans. William Watts, Vol. 2, London: William Heinemann, 1912, p. 239.

[31] Michael Stanford, *A Companion to the Study of History*, pp. 182–3.

[32] Isaac Newton, *The Mathematical Principles of Natural Philosophy*, New York: The Citadel Press, 1964, p. 17.

[33] Augustine, *Confessions*, Vol. 2, p. 275.

[34] Erwin Panofsky, 'Reflections on Historical Time', trans. Johanna Bauman, *Critical Inquiry*, Vol. 30, No.4 (Summer 2004), p. 695. Although Panofsky discussed the stylistic differences among contemporaneous works, this does not contradict the art historian's approach of conceptualising historical time through stylistic phenomena.

Riegl and his contemporaries used commonality as the unit of time in their historical narratives. Such commonalities were formed by numerous artworks that exhibited similar characteristics, and, much like Augustine's 'impressions', they served as the direct objects for contemplating the temporality model of art history. Although there is no evidence that Riegl directly adopted Augustine's views on time, we can nevertheless discern elsewhere his connection with this kind of temporal perspective. In his article on calendar illustrations, Riegl referenced Christian Ludwig Ideler's *Handbuch der mathematischen und technischen Chronologie* (1825–1826) (Figure 5).[35] In the introduction to this work, Ideler (1766–1846) wrote, 'Thus, time is neither objective nor external to us, but rather subjective – namely, a mode of imagination or a form of thought by which we can arrange things in sequence.'[36] Ideler was a colleague of August Böckh (1785–1867) at the University of Berlin. Böckh taught Max Büdinger (1828–1902), who passed on his teacher's interest in the measurement of time to his student, Riegl.[37]

In his later years, Riegl expressed his perception of the effects of time in *Der moderne Denkmalkultus* (1903) (Figure 6).[38] He discussed therein the *Alterspuren* ('age value') of monuments, describing it as manifested in their aged appearance – an effect produced by nature over time – symbolising decay and bearing the traces of passing years.[39] According to Riegl, viewers who appreciated *Alterspuren* were not nostalgic for the specific historical period the monument suggested but were, instead, captivated by the passage of time it revealed. The process of time manifested itself on the surface of the artefact, thus transforming time into a visible and even tangible object.

[35] Alois Riegl, 'Die mittelalterliche Kalenderillustration', *Mitteilungen des Instituts für Österreichische Geschichtsforschung*, X, 1889, S. 1.

[36] Ludwig Ideler, *Handbuch der mathematischen und technischen Chronologie*, Bd. 1, Berlin: August Rücker, 1825, S. 3.

[37] Michael Gubser, *Time's Visible Surface*, p. 26.

[38] Alois Riegl, *Der moderne Denkmalkultus: sein Wesen und seine Entstehung*, Wien und Leipzig: W. Braumüller, 1903; cf. 'The Modern Cult of Monuments: Its Character and Its Origin', trans. Kurt W. Forster and Diane Ghirardo, *Oppositions*, 25 (Fall 1982), pp. 21–51; 'The Modern Cult of Monuments: Its Essence and Its Development', trans. Karin Bruckner and Karen Williams, in Nicholas Stanley Price, M. Kirby Talley, Jr., and Alessandra Melucco Vaccaro (eds), Readings in Conservation: Historical and Philosophical Issues in the Conservation of Cultural Heritage, Los Angeles: Getty Conservation Institute, 1996, pp. 69–83.

[39] Alois Riegl, *Der moderne Denkmalkultus*, S. 22–4.

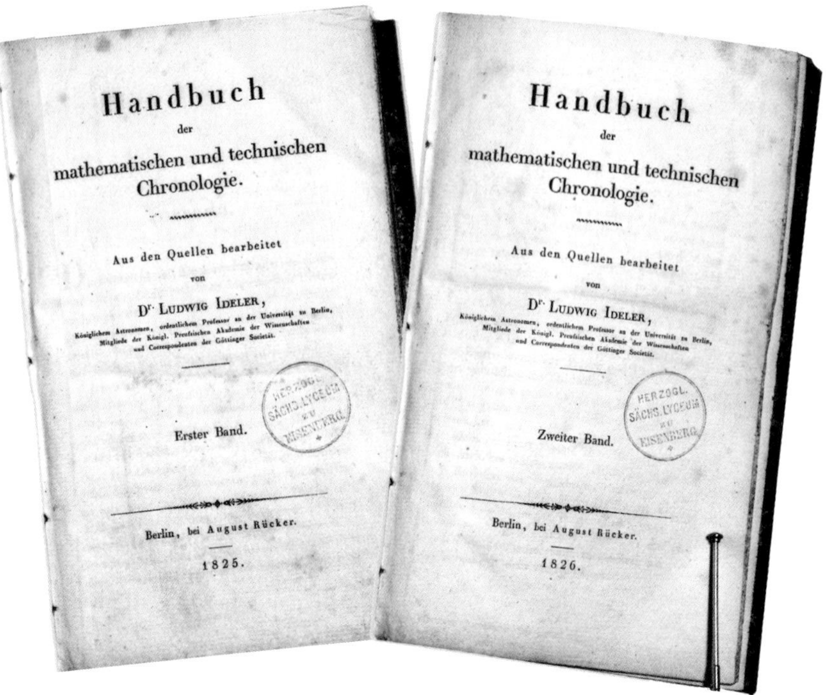

Figure 5. *Handbuch der mathematischen und technischen Chronologie I, II (1825–1826) by (Christian) Ludwig Ideler*

Because time was imperceptibly transformed into visible and tangible common elements and thereby became an entity that could be accommodated within specific developmental models that Riegl and his contemporaries , in their inquiries into the laws of artistic development, were able to overcome the limitations of the earlier conception of absolute, linear and uniform time, and instead constructed new historical frameworks by directly manipulating and these commonalities. A statement in the preface to the first edition of Heinrich Wölfflin's *Kunstgeschichtliche Grundbegriffe* reflects perfectly how linear absolute time became ineffective in art historical narratives, as *Kunstwissenschaftlers* created their own modes based on artistic commonality that conform to general laws across different periods: 'This investigation confines itself to the art of the early modern age. As much

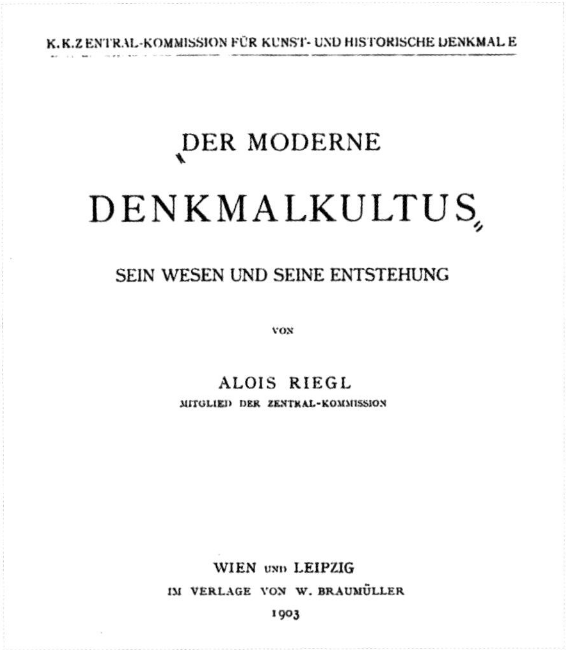

K.K.ZENTRAL-KOMMISSION FÜR KUNST- UND HISTORISCHE DENKMALE

DER MODERNE

DENKMALKULTUS

SEIN WESEN UND SEINE ENTSTEHUNG

VON

ALOIS RIEGL

MITGLIED DER ZENTRAL-KOMMISSION

WIEN UND LEIPZIG

IM VERLAGE VON W. BRAUMÜLLER

1903

Figure 6. *Der moderne Denkmalkultus* (1903) by Alois Riegl

as I am convinced that the same concepts would prove applicable to other periods as well.'[40] Clearly, Wölfflin intended to build a set of formulas for art history. In applying these formulas to explain artistic phenomena across different times and spaces, objects that were otherwise distant from one another were reassembled into a new dynamic framework, a reification with which historical narratives could engage. Edgar Wind's assessment of Wölfflin's art historical methodology confirms this observation:

> And this general formula, whose logical force undoubtedly lies in its ability to unite such contrasting phenomena under one head ... which in turn classifies as 'linear' such contrasting phenomena as Michelangelo and Holbein the Younger – this general formula is now

[40] Heinrich Wölfflin, *Principles of Art History*, p. 72. Heinrich Wölfflin, *Kunstgeschichtliche Grundbegriffe*, S. VI.

> suddenly reified as a perceptible entity with its own history. The logical tendency towards formalization ... is thus combined with a tendency towards hypostatisation which turns the formula, once it has been established, into the living subject of historical development.[41]

The aspiration to formulate the laws of art through the interrelations among commonalities is also reflected in Riegl's *Kunstgeschichte und Universalgeschichte*. He acknowledged that, beginning with the previous generation of art historians such as Franz Kugler (1808–1858), Carl Schnaase (1798–1875) and Moritz Thausing (1838–1884) to Wilhelm von Bode (1845–1929), there had already been a conscious effort to establish the rigour of art history as a discipline. They emphasised details, valued philological research and empirical visual analysis, and introduced methodologies tailored to specific types of problems, thereby advancing the professionalization of the field. However, these efforts still could not fully satisfy Riegl, as his generation of scholars sought to discover laws of art to explore the relationships between art from different periods rather than observe individual artworks in isolation. He declared that the most modern of art historians were not content with merely establishing fixed positions for great artworks in chronological order, as this failed to answer questions about their essence and origins. For him, artworks were not only distinguished by differences but were also interconnected through *gemeinsame Züge* ('common features'). Therefore, modern art historians needed to focus on these unified universal characteristics.[42] Riegl's argument is clear: observing artworks within the framework of absolute linear time cannot provide a scientific foundation for art history. Instead, he pointed to the striking similarities between the art of the second and seventeenth centuries, insisting that the perspective of *Universalgeschichte* ('universal history') is the core of art history study.[43] In this sense, it is precisely through the reification of historical time and a mode of thinking based on commonality that such anachronous connections can be

[41] Edgar Wind, 'Warburg's Concept of *Kulturwissenschaft* and its Meaning for Aesthetics', in Edgar Wind, *The Eloquence of Symbols: Studies in Humanist Art*, Oxford: Clarendon Press, 1983, p. 22.
[42] Alois Riegl, 'Kunstgeschichte und Universalgeschichte', in *Festgaben zu Ehren Max Büdinger's von seinen Freuden und Schülern*, Innsbruck: Wagner, 1898, S. 454–5.
[43] *Ibid.*, S. 455.

established, thereby opening up more possibilities for historical narratives concerning the development of art.

4. Periodicity and Continuity of the Development

Historicist thought challenged the notion of absolute laws, while *Kunstwissenschaft*, carried along by this intellectual current, began to explore the relative values of different periods and cultivate the practice of situating specific artistic commonalities within spatio-temporal coordinates. Yet, in seeking to become a systematic discipline, it eventually reverted to the old path of establishing universal laws. Nevertheless, the quest for laws propelled a transformation in art historical narrative. It no longer merely filled a diachronic sequence with successive artistic phenomena but, through the reification of time, constructed dynamic models of development in which commonalities were organized according to the theoretical logic of universal laws. When addressing the topic of 'development' in the late nineteenth and early twentieth centuries, some art historians expressed interest in periodicity and recurrence. They noticed correspondences between artworks far apart in time and space, while beneath these recurring phenomena lay an implicit continuous evolution. Through their understanding and interpretations of such phenomena, we can grasp the representative views on artistic development of that time.

When scholars of *Kunstwissenschaft* contemplated the issue of artistic development, some did so implicitly, integrating their views into case studies, while others such as Heinrich Wölfflin addressed it directly and made it an explicit point. In the conclusion of *Kunstgeschichtliche Grundbegriffe*, three subsections discuss 'The Way of the Development', 'Periodicity of the Development', and 'The Problem of New Beginnings'. In many cases, Wölfflin used the term 'development' to refer to the pattern of formal evolution (Figure 7). For example, when he stated that 'certain consistent developments can be observed in all the architectural styles of the Occident. Not only are there classical and baroque styles in the modern era and in the architecture of antiquity; they are also present on such utterly foreign soil as the Gothic.'[44] he was referring to a recurring pattern of evolution –

[44] Heinrich Wölfflin, *Principles of Art History*, p. 310.

namely, periodicity. He explained that his concern was not with the art of the sixteenth or seventeenth centuries but with 'the schema, the perceptual and expressive possibilities to which art was obliged to confine itself and to which it indeed kept in both cases'.[45] These fundamental principles, as he declared in the preface to the first edition, could be applied to other periods. Wölfflin did not stress the linear historical narrative that arranged specific artistic styles chronologically. Instead, he explained the relationships between styles through the recurring emergence of a certain developmental model.

Wickhoff and Riegl also frequently used the metaphor of *Wellen* ('waves') to describe the periodic rises and falls of artistic development. Wickhoff believed that literature and art progressed along an ascending or descending line, much like the stem of a Greek acanthus, 'which bursts forth with a new shoot, winds around itself, harboring magnificent blossoms; then it plunges into the soil, only to emerge again, beginning its splendid *Wellenspiel*'.[46] And Riegl wrote:

> Human activity must continually oscillate between extremes. Just like the wave through follows the wave crest, so too, by a necessity of nature, does todays' one sided universal historical perspective follow yesterday's one sided specialized historical view.... Between the crest and the trough of a wave lies a dead point, where the extremes touch. The fresher the creative impulses driving research, the faster it will move beyond this dead point.[47]

Therefore, how should we explain 'one of the most peculiar phenomena in art history – the ever recurring periods of revival'?[48] Wickhoff wrote "Ueber die historische Einheitlichkeit der gesamten Kunstentwicklung" (1898) for a commemorative volume dedicated to Büdinger. He advanced an assumption that artistic domains widely separated in space and time might nevertheless share a common origin. As evidence, he pointed to the meander motif on

[45] *Ibid.*, p. 305.
[46] Wilhelm Ritter von Hartel und Franz Wickhoff, *Die Wiener Genesis*, S. 14.
[47] Alois Riegl, 'Kunstgeschichte und Universalgeschichte', S. 455–6.
[48] Franz Wickhoff, 'Ueber die historische Einheitlichkeit der gesamten Kunstentwicklung', in *Festgaben zu Ehren Max Büdinger's von seinen Freuden und Schülern*, Innsbruck: Wagner, 1898, S. 469.

ABSCHLUSS

funden wurde. Darum ist die Geschichte der Malerei nicht nur nebenbei, sondern ganz wesentlich auch eine Geschichte der Dekoration.

Alle künstlerische Anschauung ist an gewisse dekorative Schemata gebunden oder — um den Ausdruck zu wiederholen — die Sichtbarkeit kristallisiert sich für das Auge unter gewissen Formen. In jeder neuen Kristallisationsform aber wird auch eine neue Seite des Weltinhalts zutage treten.

4.

Periodizität der Entwicklung

Unter diesen Umständen hat es eine große Bedeutung, daß sich in allen architektonischen Stilen des Abendlandes gewisse gleichbleibende Entwicklungen beobachten lassen. Es gibt eine Klassik und einen Barock nicht nur in der neueren Zeit und nicht nur in der antiken Baukunst, sondern auch auf einem so ganz fremdartigen Boden wie der Gotik. Trotzdem hier die Kräfterechnung eine völlig verschiedene ist, kann die Hochgotik im allgemeinsten der Formgebung doch mit den Begriffen bezeichnet werden, die wir für die klassische Kunst der Renaissance entwickelten. Sie hat einen rein „linearen" Charakter. Ihre Schönheit ist eine Flächenschönheit und ist tektonisch, insofern als auch sie das Gesetzlich-Gebundene darstellt. Das Ganze geht auf in einem System selbständiger Teile: so wenig das gotische Ideal sich deckt mit dem Ideal der Renaissance, so sind es doch lauter Teile, die eine in sich geschlossene Erscheinung besitzen, und überall ist es innerhalb dieser Formenwelt auf eine absolute Klarheit abgesehen.

Demgegenüber sucht die Spätgotik die malerischen Effekte der vibrierenden Form. Nicht im modernen Sinne, aber verglichen mit der strengen Linearität der Hochgotik ist die Form dem starr-plastischen Typ entfremdet und nach der bewegten Erscheinung hinübergedrängt worden. Der Stil entwickelt Tiefenmotive, Motive der Überschneidung wie im Ornament so im Raum. Er spielt mit dem Scheinbar-Gesetzlosen und erweicht sich stellenweise ins Fließende. Und wie nun die Rechnungen mit den Masseneffekten kommen, wo die einzelne Form nicht mehr als ganz selbständige Stimme spricht, so gefällt sich diese Kunst im Geheimnisvollen und Unübersehbaren, mit andern Worten, in einer teilweisen Verdunkelung der Klarheit.

In der Tat, wie soll man es anders nennen als barock, wenn wir — immer unter der Voraussetzung eines ganz andern Struktursystems — genau denselben Abwandlungen der Form begegnen, die wir aus der neuern Zeit kennen (vgl. die angeführten Beispiele im dritten und fünften Kapitel), bis auf die einwärtsgedrehten Fronttürme — Ingolstadt, Frauenkirche —, die die Bre-

16* 243

Figure 7. 'The Cyclical Development' in the conclusion of *Principles of Art History* (1915).

Chinese bronzes, contending that this ornament was in fact the result of Greek influence (Figure 8). Although the evidence in this essay has been proven incorrect to the extent that its argument also seems untenable, it provides insight into the principles of artistic development as Wickhoff understood them: 'Since all art derives from one common source, so much of the original must have been preserved in each of its branches that a lost thread could be found everywhere by means of which the rediscovered remains of past periods could be tied into the artistry of the present'[49] Like Riegl, Wickhoff advocated for a universal history of art. Such a universal history of art helped them incorporate seemingly recurring artistic phenomena from various times and places into a consistent system. Conversely, might it not have been precisely the presupposition of art's periodicity that provided the very logical premise for connecting ancient and modern art in their *Universalgeschichte*?

Taking the nineteenth-century Western and Far Eastern styles as examples, Wickhoff claimed that their common origin lay in Greek art. He maintained that art of other periods or regions was borrowed from the Greek tradition, which, when combined with local external factors, produced distinctive appearance while preserving its quintessence. Thus, in the resonance between classical illusionism and nineteenth-century art, he saw a self-contained cycle.[50] In other words, Wickhoff's view of the development of art history was the periodic utilisation of ancient artistic styles. Although Wickhoff had striven to rehabilitate the art of transitional periods, challenging standards of absolute beauty, the model of artistic development that he envisaged nonetheless emphasised the central position of classical norms – like a ghost from antiquity continuously reanimating itself throughout art history, assuming various guises but, ultimately, revealing its original form.

Wickhoff referred to the consistent ancient origins as *Reste* ('remains'), a concept now more commonly associated with Warburg's term *Nachleben* ('survival').[51] Wickhoff was particularly concerned with the reappearance of classical artistic forms and psychological states during the Renaissance, specifically with how gestures and movements, which Warburg later called *Pathosformeln* ('pathos formulas'), were incorporated into later art. In Wickhoff's model there was a thread of 'compelled continual imitation', in

[49] Franz Wickhoff, 'Ueber die historische Einheitlichkeit der gesamten Kunstentwicklung', S. 469. For the Enlgish translation here, see Franz Wickhoff, 'On the Historical Unity in the Universal Evolution of Art', trans. Peter Wortsman, in Gert Schiff (ed.), *German Essays on Art History*, New York: Continuum, 1988, p. 171.

[50] *Ibid.*, S. 461–9.

[51] Schlosser also mentioned this concept, using the term 'survival'. This concept was likely influenced by the anthropologist Edward Tylor (1832–1917) and his book Primitive Culture (1871); cf. Georges Didi-Huberman, *The Surviving Image: Phantoms of Time and Time of Phantoms: Aby Warburg's History of Art*, trans. Harvey L. Mendelsohn, Pennsylvania: The Pennsylvania State University Press, 2017, p. 27.

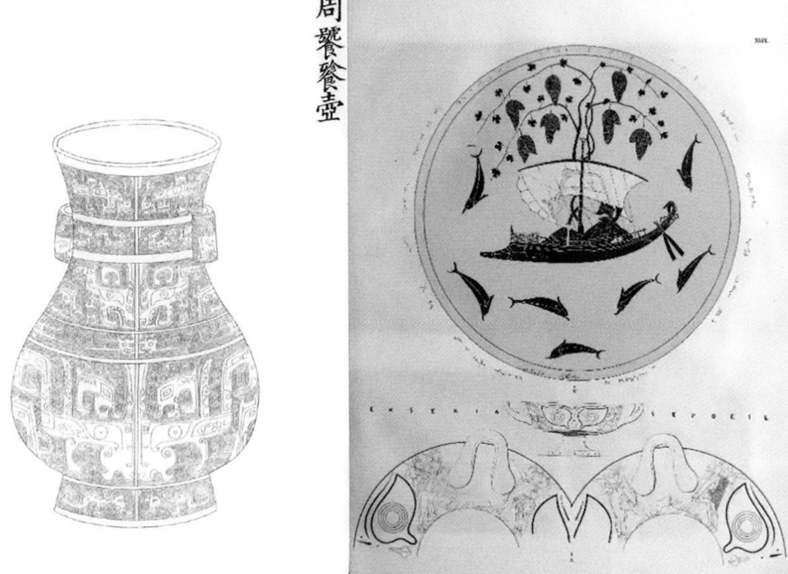

Figure 8. The taotie vessel of Hu and Dionysos cup, both illustrated in 'Ueber die historische Einheitlichkeit der gesammtenn Kunstentwicklung', Wickhoff (1898)

which even artists possessing original spirit operated within this tradition of imitation.[52] In contrast, Warburg's understanding of ancient survivals was not the passive acceptance of an inescapable tradition. For him, artists could choose whether or not to imitate certain styles – and this was entirely a conscious decision, a deliberate adaptation of artistic conventions. Or, in Warburg's own words, it was a process of *Auseinandersetzung* ('creative confrontation')[53]. Warburg's interest in the psychological expressions conveyed through gestures in images was influenced by Darwin,[54] who regarded gestures as weakened traces of past behaviours. The question of

[52] Wilhelm Ritter von Hartel und Franz Wickhoff, *Die Wiener Genesis*, S. 14.

[53] G. Bing, 'A. M. Warburg', *Journal of the Warburg and Courtauld Institutes*, Vol. 28 (1965), p. 310. August Schmarsow also employed, even before Warbug, the term 'Auseinandersetzung' in his article 'Kunstwissenschaft und Volkerpsychologie' (1907), cf. Mathew Rampley, 'Iconology of the Interval: Aby Warburg's Legacy', *Word & Image*, Vol. 17, No. 4, p. 315.

[54] cf. Aby Warburg, 'Vom Arsenal zum Laboratorium', in *Werke in einem Band*, S. 687.

how old survivals took on new forms in later periods became a key focus for art historians.

Similar to evolutionary theory, periodic recurrences in art historical developmental models typically involve questions of adaptation between old and new. In the same way as Wickhoff used the metaphor of blooming flowers to describe mature artistic styles, both Wölfflin and Riegl employed the biological characteristics of *Keim* ('germs') to demonstrate how new styles emerged from old ones – though the old styles survived through Darwinian inheritance of variation rather than pure imitation.[55] Both Riegl and Wölfflin acknowledged the uniqueness of specific art, meaning that any recurring trends or artistic features were adaptations rather than exact replications. As Wölfflin stated, 'the fact that classical art came into being at all ... this by no means goes without saying and has only occurred at certain times and particular places in the history of mankind.'[56] Likewise, when discussing historical value, Riegl argued that what we call history consisted of "everything that once was can never be again, and that everything that once was forms an irreplaceable and inextricable link in a chain of development. Or, in other words: everything that succeeds was conditioned by what came before and would not have occurred in the manner in which it did if not for those precedents. The crux of every modern historical perception is precisely the idea of development."[57] This should not be interpreted as a denial of periodic recurrence by Riegl in his later years. Both he and Wölfflin emphasised the uniqueness of specific phenomena as historical links without questioning the recurrence of artistic development patterns or visual

[55] 'Nur verzahnt sich eben Altes und Neues hier so, daß es schwer ist, den Schnitt zu machen. Wie denn die Historiker immer wieder schwanken, wo sie das Kapitel von der neueren Kunstgeschichte beginnen lassen sollen. Mit strengen Ansprüchen an die „Reinlichkeit" der Periodenteilungen kommt man nicht weiter. In der alten Form ist die neue schon enthalten, wie neben dem welkenden Laub der Keim des jungen schon da ist.' (Heinrich Wölfflin, *Kunstgeschichtliche Grundbegriffe*, S. 247). 'Wenn sie sich hie und da dennoch entschloss, ein solches Spätwerk zu behandeln, so geschah es in der Regel um des antiquarisch-historischen Inhaltes und nicht um der künstlerischen Form willen. Begegnet man aber einmal einer Ausnahme, so gieng sie gewiss von einem Forscher aus, dessen Interesse für die bildende Kunst an der Grenze der Classik nicht Halt macht, und ihn dadurch in Stand setzt, selbst an den Werken der spätesten Antike, inmitten der Zeichen des Absterbens und der Verwesung, die Keime neuen Werdens und Blühens zu erkennen.' (Alois Riegl, Die Spätrömische Kunstindustrie, Wien: Kaiserlich-Königlichen Hof- und Staatsdruckerei, 1901, S. 2).

[56] Heinrich Wölfflin, *Principles of Art History*, p. 308.

[57] Alois Riegl, 'The Modern Cult of Monuments: Its Essence and Its Development', p. 70.

patterns. What concerned them more was the process of 'determination', or 'adaptation', that these specific phenomena underwent to become what they were, thereby forming the patterns of development that made recurrence possible.

Unfortunately, Wölfflin ultimately failed to provide a convincing explanation for the causes of development.[58] Nevertheless, at least, he depicted honestly the pattern of artistic development; in many respects, his developmental model aligned with Riegl's views. In practice, both Wölfflin and Riegl preset their own categories and then sought correspondences among various artistic phenomena. For example, Wölfflin's categories consisted of five pairs of concepts. By claiming to classify based on results while simultaneously asserting that unclear forms 'are best accommodated in the realm of impressionistic, painterly apprehension', he risked falling into circular reasoning.[59] Riegl's concept of *Kunstwollen* was regarded as the determining factor in the development of stylistic phenomena. In Riegl's view, the *Kunstwollen* of a specific period dictated the appearance of art at that time. He made no attempt to conceal the teleological nature of this concept, stating in *Stilfragen* that he first introduced 'a teleological approach by recognizing the art work as the result of a definite and purposeful *Kunstwollen* which makes its way forward in the struggle with function, raw material, and technique'.[60] That is to say, a particular change emerged at a particular moment because it aligned with the *Kunstwollen* of that time, while incompatible elements remained dormant until they were later activated by the *Kunstwollen* in the future.[61] While Riegl seemingly used *Kunstwollen* to offer a definitive explanation for the driving forces behind artistic development, both he and Wölfflin could classify and describe only those phenomena that had already

[58] In the introduction to the English edition of *Kunstgeschichtliche Grundbegriffe*, Evonne Levy expressed a similar view. Evonne Levy, 'Wölfflin's *Principles of Art History* (1915–2015): A Prolegomenon for Its Second Century', in *Principles of Art History*, p. 13.

[59] '... im Bereich einer impressionistisch-malerischen Auffassung am besten unterkommen'. Heinrich Wölfflin, *Kunstgeschichtliche Grundbegriffe*, S. 238. For the English translation here, see Heinrich Wölfflin, *Principles of Art History*, p. 306.

[60] Alois Riegl, *Late Roman Art Industry*, p. 9; also cf. Otto Pächt, 'Art Historians and Art Critics-vi: Alois Riegl', *The Burlington Magazine*, Vol. 105, No. 722 (May 1963), p. 190.

[61] Marsha Morton, 'Art's "Contest with Nature": Darwin, Haeckel, and the Scientific Art History of Alois Riegl', in Barbara Larson and Sabine Flach (eds), *Darwin and Theories of Aesthetics and Cultural History*, Surrey: Ashgate, 2013, p. 59.

occurred. As Wölfflin himself admitted, 'one only sees what one is looking for, but then one only looks for what one can see.'[62]

In the preface to the sixth edition of *Principles of Art History*, Wölfflin wrote that 'It is safe to say that a specific point in history can never be revisited, but it is just as true to say that individual, self-contained developments can be distinguished within the one overall development and that the developmental lines of these periods evidence a certain parallelism.'[63] In the conclusion, he presented two possible explanations for the causes of artistic change. One was 'the result of an internal development, a development that, as it were, occurs of its own accord within the perceptual apparatus'; the other was 'an external impulse that determines the transformation, the changed interest, the altered attitude toward the world'. His conclusion encompassed both. The internal and external causes operated simultaneously: the internal modes of seeing preexisted, but their development and the direction they took depended on external factors.[64] Riegl's *Kunstwollen* was an internal driving force shared by all humans, yet it varied according to external factors such as nation, location and time.[65] He argued that 'Natural objects reveal themselves to the human sense of sight as isolated figures, yet simultaneously as connected with the universe into an infinite whole. They are bounded by principles, but they merge more or less fluidly into their surroundings. They present a closed local character while also participate in the overall tone of their environment. It is upon this dual appearance of natural phenomena in the eyes of humans that the development of huaman *Kunstwollen* is based.'[66] Here, Wölfflin and Riegl reached a remarkable consensus: A pre-existing form or force is handed down through generations along the mainstream of artistic evolution. When stimulated by external factors, it rises to the surface; otherwise, it continues to flow as undercurrents. Each time it emerges, like a cresting wave, it is never exactly the same as before.

[62] Heinrich Wölfflin, *Principles of Art History*, p. 309.
[63] Heinrich Wölfflin, *Principles of Art History*, p. 79.
[64] Heinrich Wölfflin, *Principles of Art History*, p. 255–256.
[65] Alois Riegl, *Late Roman Art Industry*, p. 231.
[66] Alois Riegl, 'Naturwerk und Kunstwerk', in *Gesammelte Aufsätze*, Ausburg: Dr. Benno Filser Verlag, 1928, S. 60.

At least since Schnaase, there was a view that regarded artistic development as a continuous and progressive process.[67] Under the influence of Darwin's theory of evolution, the progression of human culture from barbarism to civilisation was described and interpreted as a process of maturation that could be explained through psychological science.[68] In a book discussing evolution theory and art history, Matthew Rampley argued that Gottfried Semper (1803–1879), Wickhoff, Riegl, and Max Dvořák (1874–1921) all treated art history as an evolutionary process. Wölfflin and Riegl considered art as an indicator of visual evolution, while Warburg constructed art history through the evolution of human emotions and aesthetic responses.[69] I do not intend here to delve into the progressive view of art history, nor do I plan to discuss the distinction between evolution as a value judgment and a relatively neutral process of advancement; that would require a separate study.[70] However, it is worth noting that the continuity of development in art history is a significant and universal issue in *Kunstwissenschaft*.

As previously mentioned, Wickhoff's history of artistic development was essentially a repeated utilisation of the same ancient source, uninterrupted not only in time but also in space, as he attempted to unite Eastern and Western art. This continuity enabled the rehabilitation of supposedly declining transitional periods. Riegl and Wölfflin expressed a similar view that artistic development was a process that could be observed to be continuous. Wölfflin called for 'an art history that can trace, step by step, the emergence of modern vision'.[71] Twenty-two years earlier, in the preface to *Stilfragen*, Riegl, responding to extremists who had questioned whether ornament even had a history, reminded readers that from the foundation of art history as a discipline, scholars had already considered

[67] 'Es genügt uns zu wissen, dass wir in dem Entwickelungsgange der Kunst auch das treueste Bild der fortschreitenden Humanität haben', Carl Schnaase, *Geschichte der bildenden Künste*, Düsseldorf: Verlag von Julius Buddeus, 1843, S. 88–9.

[68] Gombrich, E. H., 'Aby Warburg: His Aims and Methods', in *The Shapes of Art History I*, p. 445.

[69] Matthew Rampley, *The Seductions of Darwin: Art, Evolution, Neuroscience*, University Park: Penn State University Press, 2017, p. 7.

[70] In fact, in an article discussing the progression of art history, Ján Bakoš stated that Riegl 'replaced the idea of history conceived of as a progressive process by an idea of history conceived of as never-ceasing stream of equal changes' (Ján Bakoš, 'The Vienna School's Views of the Structure of the Art Historical Process', in *Wien und die Entwicklung der kunsthistorischen Methode*, Wien, Köln, Graz: Hermann Böhlaus Nachfolger, 1984, p. 117.

[71] Heinrich Wölfflin, *Kunstgeschichtliche Grundbegriffe*, S. V.

purely ornamental forms from the perspective of 'progressive development'.[72] In his later works, such as *Die Spätrömische Kunstindustrie* (1901) and *Das holländische Gruppenporträt* (1902), Riegl demonstrated the continuity of art progression. He argued that art history consisted of continuous phases, each stage having its own internal purpose for change while simultaneously existing within a continual, universal development.[73]

Riegl's developmental model cannot be summarised as simply teleological, nor is it purely cyclical or progressive – yet it possesses all these characteristics simultaneously. In the process of development, he identified forms tracing back to the past, but these were not exact imitations of previous ones. With a historicist attitude, he situated each form at a unique intersection of time and space, explaining the emergence of new styles through partial teleology (*Kunstwollen*). Keith Moxey also noted that both Wölfflin and Riegl equated Hegel's Phenomenology of Spirit with the concept of style, tracing its teleological driving force through time.[74] Thus, Riegl's developmental model seems to be described as a combination of evolutionary innovation and continuous adaptation.[75] Bakoš considered this continuous evolution of art and the sharp changes in style to be an antithetical idea within Riegl's historical perspective.[76] Similarly, Wölfflin stated, 'individual, self-contained developments can be distinguished within the one overall development and that the developmental lines of these periods evidence a certain parallelism.'[77] In the developmental models of art history proposed by Riegl and Wölfflin, the specialised studies of individual cases undertaken by their predecessors was, for the first time, integrated with the aspiration to establish a universal history of art.

5. Does Art History Need a Theory of Development?

Kunstwissenschaft was neither an academic school nor the formal designation of a specific research; rather, it may be described as an academic ideal that

[72] Alois Riegl, *Stilfragen*, S. V.
[73] Michael Gubser, *Time's Visible Surface*, p. 161.
[74] Keith Moxey, *Visual Time: The Image in History*, Durham and London: Duke University Press, 2013, p. 25.
[75] Michael Gubser, *Time's Visible Surface*, p.161.
[76] Ján Bakoš, 'The Vienna School's Views of the Structure of the Art Historical Process', p. 118.
[77] Heinrich Wölfflin, *Principles of Art History*, p. 79.

emerged within art history as a discipline in the nineteenth century. Driven by this ideal, several classic works were produced around the turn of the twentieth century that have profoundly influenced the landscape of art history research up to the present day. Although these works of art history adopted different themes and methods, they shared a common goal: to encompass artistic phenomena from various periods and regions within universal modes of historical development and to connect the inherent relationships between these phenomena through basic principles. We have traced the theoretical background from which these developmental models emerged, particularly the changes in the understanding of historical time.

First, time as a fundamental category was incorporated into philosophical discussions. Secondly, influenced by psychology, physiology and aesthetics, the viewer's mode of visual perception replaced artworks as objects to become the research focus of *Kunstwissenschaft*. Thus, studying the evolution of artistic styles became an investigation into different subjective cognitive types along the chain of time. Furthermore, historicism distrusted eternally valid rational laws and emphasised the position of things in specific times and spaces, creating an attitude of relativism that resonated with *Kunstwissenschaftlers'* rejection of absolute value standards and facilitated the construction of a new art historical order. Finally, a philosophy of Hegelianism, which linked cultural phenomena, including art, to specific *Zeitgeists*, paved the way for *Kunstwissenschaftlers* to employ certain artistic commonalities as units of historical time. Under these combined influences, the focus of art history shifted from individual artworks and artists to the overall characteristics of art itself, from the particular to the universal, and from specific historical facts to the pursuit of universal laws in *Kunstwissenschaft*. Artistic commonalities, conditioned by time and space, contributed to shaping the developmental trajectory of art history, replacing the chronological accumulation of events. This shift also rendered less significant the concept of absolute time as a measuring scale. Instead, the commonalities reflected in artworks with similar traits became the units of time for constructing historical narratives by *Kunstwissenschaft*, thus reifying time. When *Kunstwissenschaftlers* contemplated the laws of artistic development, they were essentially manipulating reified time to fill their historical structures based on internal logical development.

These shifts in the understanding of historical time facilitated the creation of non-linear developmental models, allowing art historians to highlight and capture the scientific universal laws of art history, whether through asynchronous or synchronous narratives, while *Kunstwissenschaftlers* incorporated periodic recurring artistic phenomena from different times and places into a universal development history through laws of art history or basic concepts. However, their laws of art were derived from what had already occurred, creating a gap between their developmental models and the universal applicability they sought to achieve.

Should there then be a concept of development in art history? Contemporary scholars rarely discuss this question, perhaps partly due to the increasing subdivision and specialisation of disciplines. Back in their time, Riegl and his contemporaries were dissatisfied with the research focus of art history being limited to scientific case analysis and were determined to explore the universal logic of artistic development. However, debates on this issue continued at least through the twentieth century. Gombrich, a steadfast opponent of historical determinism, remained critical of laws of artistic development based on Hegelianism. In contrast, Otto Pächt (1902–1988), as an heir to the Vienna School of Art History, defended the modes of historical development of his predecessors, candidly presenting the dilemmas faced by both sides:

> The historian who tries to infuse some meaning into his work all too easily finds himself facing an awkward dilemma. If he simply registers a sequence of events, his presentation risks declining into a lifeless, piecemeal enumeration. But, if he seeks to understand those events and the order in which they occurred, to explain this to himself and to others as a significant or even an intrinsically inevitable process – if he goes further and detects an evolutionary logic at work – he at once lays himself open to the accusation that he is a theologian in disguise, one whose belief in the inevitability of an ultimate evolutionary

> destination lends currency to an educationally and socially dangerous fatalism.[78]

Art historians of the late nineteenth and early twentieth centuries attempted to develop a speculative system grounded in empirical foundations. This combination of objectivity and subjectivity, along with their appeal to modes of historical development, reflected the complex academic landscape and anxieties of the discipline in their time. While inheriting their predecessors' scientific attitude of positivism in handling individual cases at the micro level, they urgently needed universal laws at the macro level to secure the disciplinary status of art history, ensure its interpretability, and establish connections among various artistic phenomena. To put it in a historicist tone, they attempt to construct the developmental logic of art history was a choice made in response to the problems of their time.

[78] Otto Pächt, *The Practice of Art History: Reflections on Method*, trans. David Britt, London: Harvey Miller Publishers, 1999, p. 118.

II

EXPERIENCE AND TRANSCENDENCE: FUNDAMENTAL QUESTIONS OF *KUNSTWISSENSCHAFT*

As already observed, the generation of art historians represented by Wickhoff, Riegl and Wölfflin was not satisfied with the overly specialised research perspectives of their predecessors. Instead, they sought laws of artistic development, attempting thereby to establish connections among various artistic phenomena through common categories. They aimed to address questions about the essence and origins of art and explain the causes of stylistic changes. However, strictly speaking, they failed to fully achieve their goals, and their primary work more closely resembled observing shifts in visual perception patterns through classification. Their unfinished work prompted the next generation of scholars to reflect on the issues of art history, not only approaching their teachers' solutions with caution but also even proposing new objectives for *Kunstwissenschaft*. Based on earlier studies, we can focus on several representatives of those young scholars and their academic ideas to reveal the aspirations of *Kunstwissenschaft* in its final phase and to elucidate the logic behind the methodological shifts in art history research in the early twentieth century.

1. From Part to Whole

As a concept, *Kunstwissenschaft* can be described, but it is difficult to define, as its connotations and objectives evolved alongside the development of art studies in the nineteenth century. From the establishment of art history as an academic discipline to the emergence of the Vienna School in the early twentieth century, the development of *Kunstwissenschaft* in the field of art history can be roughly divided into three phases. However, it must be noted that this division is neither strict nor theoretical; it serves merely narrative purposes. These stages overlap in time and, thus, can also be understood as three guiding principles or research trends in *Kunstwissenschaft*.

In his review of the Vienna school of Art History, Julius von Schlosser regarded Rudolf Eitelberger as its 'Heros Ktistes'.[1] This generation brought scientific features to art history, primarily manifested in their analysis and categorisation of artworks with the attitudes of natural science and consciously departing from the romantic style of art writing. Eitelberger based 'his academic instruction on the individual artifact in technical, historical terms, and thereby escaped the danger of theoretical ramblings.'[2] The close connection between museums and universities at that time also reflected the implementation of this academic principle. His successors – Thausing, Wickhoff and, later, Riegl – effectively maintained this tradition of positivist research. Of course, this was not unique to the Vienna School. Since the Italian physician Giovanni Morelli (1816–1891) began 'diagnosing' artworks, empirical research methods had already been laying the scientific foundation for art history.[3] Furthermore, the philological work on primary art sources in the nineteenth century should also be viewed as a product guided by this scientific spirit. The adoption of attitudes and methods from natural science in the study of art was the foundation of *Kunstwissenschaft*. However, the subsequent shift in its internal objectives was partly driven by an anxiety over its subordinate disciplinary status. Art history was once considered in European universities to be a secondary discipline within the humanities or philosophy. Riegl, in arguing that art should be interpreted from within, contributed to art history's establishment as a genuinely independent discipline.[4] Thus, the next generation of *Kunstwissenschaftlers* undertook the mission of securing the disciplinary autonomy of art history.

The positivist approach stresses factual evidence, attempting to identify the contextual and conditioning factors, including artistic intentions, techniques, stylistic elements, the circumstances of production, among others. However, Venturi detected an aversion to philosophy in this positivist academic faith. Its drawback, he argued, lay in excluding thought,

[1] Julius von Schlosser, 'The Vienna School of the History of Art – Review of a Century of Austrian Scholarship in German', translated and edited by Karl Johns, *Journal of Art Historiography*, No.1 (December 2009), p. 10.

[2] Julius von Schlosser, 'The Vienna School of the History of Art', p. 10.

[3] E.H. Gombrich, 'Kunstwissenschaft', in *Atlantisbuch der Kunst,* Zürich: Atlantis – Verlag, 1952, S. 654.

[4] Rolf Winkes, 'Foreword', p. XXI.

whether philosophical or historical, from the study of art. These philologists in the field of art history, being unable to make 'an historical reconstruction or a critical judgment of art', made the achievements of art philology 'very much more like an imposing mound of stones than an architecture in stone'.[5]

The pursuit of thoughtful interpretation prompted the second generation of *Kunstwissenschaftlers*, represented by Wickhoff, Riegl and Wölfflin, to forge a distinct path from their predecessors. They were no longer content with merely constructing a partial knowledge of art history piece by piece. Rather, they strove to explain the universal principles of artistic development, thereby providing art history with a theoretical framework for its autonomy. This does not mean that the importance of empiricism was significantly diminished; it remained the foundation for the scientific nature of modern art history. However, at this stage, *Kunstwissenschaftlers* also sought to draw insights from other fields such as philosophy, psychology, biology and sociology, aiming by so doing to comprehend the essence of representation from a more macro-level perspective and explain the secrets of artistic development. Both Wölfflin's five pairs of concepts and Riegl's antithesis of haptic and optic reflected their approach of incorporating scientific classifications into specific developmental models based on a certain hierarchy of values.[6]

The study of art shifted towards a 'history of art without names'. Wölfflin and Riegl shared a common approach in suggesting universal laws of stylistic change through their descriptions of visual cognitive patterns. However, although Wölfflin declared in his first book that his aim was to 'discover in the "capriciousness and the return to chaos" a law which would vouchsafe one an insight into the intimate workings of art. This, I confess, is to me the real aim of art history', he placed significant emphasis on the relationship between stylistic phenomena and cultural unity. He believed that 'to explain a style then can mean nothing other than to place it in its general historical context and to verify that it speaks in harmony with the other organs of its age.'[7] Riegl, by contrast, deliberately highlighted the autonomy of art in his explanation of artistic

[5] Lionello Venturi, *History of Art Criticism*, pp. 216-217.

[6] Margaret Olin, *Forms of Representation in Alois Riegl's Theory of Art*, p. xviii.

[7] Heinrich Wölfflin, *Renaissance and Baroque*, trans. Kathrin Simon, Ithaca, New York: Cornell University Press, 1964, "Preface the First Edition", p. 79.

development. While Riegl, like Wölfflin, drew on methodologies from other disciplines, he explained the autonomous evolution of style through his concept of *Kunstwollen*. It is widely known that Gombrich classified several prominent art historians, including Riegl, within the Hegelian tradition, exposing their reliance on *Zeitgeist* to determine the evolution of form.[8] However, Riegl never claimed explicitly that artistic creation was a product of overall culture; he merely acknowledged external environmental influences. Like Schnasse, his concept of *Kunstwollen* emphasised the direct determining factors of the human spirit in artistic creation, leading some to suggest that Riegl had returned to Romantic art theory in this aspect.[9] After encountering Adolf von Hildebrand's (1847–1921) theory, Wölfflin also revised his earlier views – acknowledging that *formale Momente* ('formal elements') could not simply emerge from the atmosphere of an era – as a rejection of the core views of Renaissance and Baroque. The development of form, or ways of viewing was sufficient as the central focus of art history research. Wölfflin wrote, 'This concerns development that repeats everywhere,' referring to a regularity in the evolution of form. Moreover, development implied 'integration and differentiation', which Gombrich summarised as the solution to *einer künstlerischen Aufgabe* ('an artistic task').[10]

At this stage, the second generation of *Kunstwissenschaftlers* achieved two significant outcomes: they proposed new models for the development of art history; and, through the strong intervention of conceptual and formal category, they distilled the unique essential questions of artistic activity, thereby establishing art history's distinctive position within the humanities. While the first generation of *Kunstwissenschaftlers* had brought a positivist scientific approach to art history research, thus providing basic information about artworks as human-made artefacts within their historical contexts, their successors clearly recognised the self-sufficient nature of art, independent of other aspects. Wölfflin and Riegl and their contemporaries approached this core attribute of art indirectly and subtly through formal analysis, while the younger generation chose to engage directly in philosophical discussions.

[8] E.H. Gombrich, 'In Search of Cultural History', p. 44.
[9] Rolf Winkes, 'Foreword', p. XIX.
[10] E.H. Gombrich, 'Kunstwissenschaft', p. 659.

2. From the External to the Internal

What I refer to as the third generation of *Kunstwissenschaftlers* generally comprises students of the second generation, and my discussion focuses primarily on Panofsky, Wind and the so-called Vienna School. These scholars recognised the theoretical limitations of their predecessors, and they strove to advance their work to a deeper and purer level. Before the Second World War, they published numerous papers exploring theories of art history, including both critiques of and improvements on their predecessors' work, and outlooks and even manifestos regarding future methodologies. Yet, they all converged on one fundamental question: What is the essence of art history research? Or, more specifically, What are the foundational questions of art studies? In the process of answering these questions, we witness the late stage of *Kunstwissenschaft*'s development, marked by a transition from the empirical to the transcendental.

Three papers are particularly significant in Panofsky's early theoretical writings on art history. The first, published in 1915, responded to Wölfflin's 'Problem of Styles';[11] the second, published in 1920, addressed Riegl's concept of *Kunstwollen*;[12]and the third, five years later, explored the foundational system of concepts in art theory and discussed fundamental questions in artistic creation. This third paper, 'Über das Verhältnis der Kunstgeschichte zur Kunsttheorie', was published in 1925 in *Zeitschrift für Ästhetik und allgemeine Kunstwissenschaft* (Figure 9).[13] Panofsky's student,

[11] Erwin Panofsky, 'Das Problem des Stils in der bildenden Kunst', *Zeitschrift für* Ästhetik *und allgemeine Kunstwissenschaft*, 10 (1915), S. 460–67. On 7 December 1911, Wölfflin delivered a lecture, '*Das Problem des Stils in der bildenden Kunst*', at the Königlich-Preußische Akademie der Wissenschaften. The manuscript of the lecture was published in *Sitzungsberichte der königlich preußischen Akademie der Wissenschaften* in 1912. Four years later, Panofsky gave his article the same title – a challenging decision.

[12] Erwin Panofsky, 'Der Begriff des Kunstwollens', *Zeitschrift für Ästhetik und allgemeine Kunstwissenschaft*, 14 (1920), S. 321–39.

[13] Erwin Panofsky, 'Über das Verhältnis der Kunstgeschichte zur Kunsttheorie: Ein Beitrag zu der Erörtung über die Moglichkeit kunstwissenschaftlicher Grundbegriffe', *Zeitschrift für* Ästhetik *und allgemeine Kunstwissenschaft*, 18 (1925), S. 129–61. (Panofsky's Grundbegriffe was different from Wölfflin's.) This article was later included in the collection *Aufsätze zu Grundfragen der Kunstwissenschaft*, edited by Hariolf Oberer and Egon Verheyen, Berlin: Verlag Bruno Hessling, 1964, pp. 49–75. It was reprinted in *Deutschsprachige Aufsätze*, edited by Karen Michels and Martin Warnke, Berlin: Akademie Verlag, 1998, pp. 1019–34. The English version, titled '*On the Relationship of Art History and Art Theory: Towards the Possibility of a Fundamental System of Concepts for a Science of Art*', translated by Katharina Lorenz and Jaś Elsner, was published in *Critical Inquiry, Vol. 35, No. 1 (Autumn 2008)*, pp. 43–71.

Wind, also published an article, 'Zur Systematik der künstlerischen Probleme' (Figure 10), in the same issue.[14] Although Panofsky emphasised *Grundbegriffe* ('conceptual system') in the subtitle, he pointed out in the main text that *künstlerische Probleme* ('artistic problems'), articulated by the fundamental concepts of *Kunstwissenschaft*, were of indispensable importance.[15] In short, both of them critically identified the inadequacies of earlier art history research on a theoretical level, focusing on the concept of *künstlerische Probleme*.

VII.

Über das Verhältnis der Kunstgeschichte zur Kunsttheorie.

Ein Beitrag zu der Erörterung über die Möglichkeit „kunstwissenschaftlicher Grundbegriffe".

Von

Erwin Panofsky.

In einer vor mehreren Jahren erschienenen Arbeit[1]) hat der Verfasser dieses Aufsatzes den Versuch gemacht, den in der gegenwärtigen Kunstwissenschaft häufig verwendeten, aber nicht immer zutreffend bestimmten Begriff des »Kunstwollens« (mit welchem Terminus wir seit Alois Riegl die Summe oder Einheit der in irgend einem künstlerischen Phänomen[2]) sich offenbarenden schöpferischen Kräfte zu bezeichnen pflegen) einigermaßen zu klären. Dieser Versuch hatte sich um den Nachweis bemüht, daß jenes »Kunstwollen«, wenn anders die Untersuchung nicht einem *circulus vitiosus* verfallen solle, nicht psychologistisch als Wille des Künstlers (oder der Epoche usw.) gedeutet werden dürfe, vielmehr nur dann einen möglichen Gegenstand kunstwissenschaftlicher Erkenntnis darstelle, wenn es nicht als psychologische »Wirklichkeit«, sondern als ein metempirischer Gegenstand betrachtet werde — als etwas, das als »immanenter Sinn« im künstlerischen Phänomene »liegt«. In dieser Eigenschaft — und nur in dieser Eigenschaft — erschien uns das »Kunstwollen« mit Hilfe a priori gültiger »Grundbegriffe« faßbar, d. h. also als ein Denkgegenstand, der überhaupt nicht in einer Wirklichkeitssphäre (auch nicht in der Sphäre historischer Wirklichkeit) anzutreffen ist, sondern, mit Husserl zu reden, »eidetischen« Charakter trägt.

Der kritische Teil dieser Ausführungen scheint, soweit uns bisher Äußerungen zu dem genannten Aufsatz bekannt geworden sind, keinem

[1]) Zeitschr. f. Ästhetik u. allgem. Kunstwissensch. XIV, 1920, S. 320 ff.

[2]) Unter der Bezeichnung »künstlerisches Phänomen« oder »künstlerische Erscheinung« verstehen wir hier und im folgenden jedes kunstwissenschaftliche Objekt, das unter dem Gesichtspunkt der Stilkritik als eine Einheit betrachtet werden kann — sei diese Einheit nun regional (Volksstil), epochal (Zeitstil), oder personal (Individualstil) begrenzt, oder sei sie nur durch ein einzelnes Kunstwerk repräsentiert.

Zeitschr. f. Ästhetik u. allg. Kunstwissenschaft. XVIII 9

Figure 9. 'Über das Verhältnis der Kunstgeschichte zur Kunsttheorie', Panofsky (1925)

[14] Edgar Wind, 'Zur Systematik der künstlerischen Probleme', *Zeitschrift für* Ästhetik *und allgemeine Kunstwissenschaft*, 18 (1925), S. 438–86. This article was adapted from his doctoral dissertation, *Ästhetischer und kunstwissenschaftlicher Gegenstand: ein Beitrag zur Methodologie der Kunstgeschichte* (1922), which was republished by Philo Verlag in 2012.

[15] Erwin Panofsky, 'Über das Verhältnis der Kunstgeschichte zur Kunsttheorie', S. 149.

XVI.

Zur Systematik der künstlerischen Probleme[1]).

Von

Edgar Wind.

A. Der Begriff des »künstlerischen Problems« und seine Anwendung in der Kunstgeschichte.

I.

Es gibt kaum einen kunstwissenschaftlichen Terminus, der häufiger mißbraucht würde als der des »künstlerischen Problems«, — keinen, der mit stärkeren Unklarheiten behaftet wäre. Man hat sich gewöhnt, derjenigen Art der Kunstgeschichtsforschung, für die Wölfflin den Ausdruck »Kunstgeschichte ohne Namen« geprägt hat, den positiveren und zugleich anspruchsvolleren Titel »Problemgeschichte« zu leihen. Dabei hat ein großer Teil der von Wölfflin gestellten Forderungen mit einer Untersuchung von »Problemen« (im eigentlichen Sinne des Wortes) noch gar nichts zu tun. Wer die Wandlungen »der Licht- und Schattenbehandlung, der Perspektive und Raumdarstellung« verfolgt, wer den Wechsel »in der Figurenzeichnung, Gewandzeichnung, Baumzeichnung« aufweist, der befaßt sich noch lediglich mit den Gestalteigenschaften des Kunstwerks, mit den Merkmalen seiner äußeren Erscheinung. Ähnlich wie der Botaniker, verfährt er morphologisch beschreibend und vergleichend; wenn er auch die Objekte nicht, wie dieser, klassenweise nach Gattungen und Arten, sondern reihenweise im Sinne einer zeitlichen Abfolge ordnet. So notwendig und unentbehrlich aber diese Art der Betrachtung für den Fortgang der kunstwissenschaftlichen Urteilsbildung ist — (jede Untersuchung von Problemen hat von ihr auszugehen und muß sich letzten Endes auf sie berufen können) —, mit den Problemen selbst kommt sie noch gar nicht in unmittelbare Berührung. Denn die Erscheinungen als solche sind noch keine »Probleme«; diese beginnen vielmehr erst dort, wo an die Stelle der bloßen »Schilderung« die »Deutung« tritt.

[1]) Der Aufsatz ist einer größeren Arbeit (»Ästhetischer und kunstwissenschaftlicher Gegenstand«) entnommen, die im Juli 1922 abgeschlossen wurde, aber aus äußeren Gründen noch nicht erscheinen kann.

Figure 10. 'Zur Systematik der künstlerischen Probleme', Wind, (1925)

As previously discussed, earlier art historians such as Riegl and Wölfflin had sought to reveal the laws of artistic development and categorise stylistic phenomena through specific theoretical categories. However, ultimately, they failed to explain the causes of stylistic changes. Panofsky, at least, expressed regret about this, believing that describing artworks merely through *sinnliche Eigenschaften* ('sensible qualities') was too superficial. He argued that art history research required more profound concepts to summarise stylistic characteristics and interpret the sensible qualities, thereby revealing the underlying *Gestaltungsprinzipien* ('principles of design'). In other words, classification based on *sinnliche Eigenschaften* merely connected artworks that appeared similar in dimensions, materials, colours, style or other sensory aspects. This belonged to the *eine untere Schicht* ('lower layer') of art history concepts, which were demonstrative rather than explanatory. Describing sensible qualities did not mean describing the style. Only the *eine obere Schicht* ('upper layer') of concepts could address the essential *Stilkriterien* ('stylistic criteria').[16] Panofsky criticised artistic judgements that remained confined to the level of phenomenonal experience. He singled out a negative example in a footnote:

> Heinrich Wölfflin's categories are subject to the objection that they aim to reduce not the arising of the problem but the solution of the problem into one formula and hence to bring the theoretical antithesis of metempirical values into the empirical world of historical reality. They thus take an intermediate position that can be attacked from both sides. Studied as fundamental concepts of a theory of art they do not fulfil the requirement that they be legitimated a priori and that their object be beyond the world of manifestation; studied as concepts of art historical characterization they fail to fulfil the requirement to come to terms with the diversity of artistic phenomena because they restrict the wealth of such phenomena into one system of absolute contrasts, which even in itself is not without contradiction, by the way.[17]

While the title suggests that Pan's essay examines the relationship between art history and art theory, his actual claim is that art history is unworkable in the absence of art theory. One of the tasks of art history is to distil the stylistic characteristics of artworks, which requires concepts that can describe stylistic features in an epistemological sense. These concepts, however, do not refer to Wölfflin's five famous antitheses. Panofsky argued that concepts describing sensible qualities alone cannot summarise style; they can only serve as a basis for describing stylistic characteristics. In other words, the

[16] Erwin Panofsky, 'Über das Verhältnis der Kunstgeschichte zur Kunsttheorie', S. 149. Note: all subsequent references consult the English translations, while page numbers corresponding to the original German text, except for block quotations, which are cited with the page numbers of the English translation.

[17] Erwin Panofsky, '*On the Relationship of Art History and Art Theory*'. p. 52.

categories proposed by Wölfflin still fail to get to the heart of the matter. Art historians can only define the empirical manifestations of art, but they did not provide solutions to *künstlerische Probleme.*[18]

What, then, was the attitude of Wind, Panofsky's student, towards Wölfflin? At the beginning of 'Zur Systematik der künstlerischen Probleme', Wind pointed out that there were many misunderstandings about *künstlerische Probleme*. Wölfflin's phrase of 'art history without names' was often regarded as a *Problemgeschichte* ('history of problems'). But, in fact, Wölfflin never investigated genuine 'problems'. Wind's reasoning for this judgement was essentially identical to that of his teacher: this kind of art history merely engaged in *Schilderung* ('description'), not *Deutung* ('interpretation'). He observed that some scholars pursued changes in 'light and shade, perspective, and spatial representation', while others distinguished the depiction of 'figures, drapery, and trees'. However, what they focused on were just the formal characteristics with the nature of external *Erscheinung* ('appearance') in artworks. This, Wind argued, was akin to the work of botanists who produced only morphological descriptions and comparisons. Wind acknowledged that such observations were indispensable for advancing the evaluation of art science, but they never directly addressed any problems. External appearances alone, he insisted, did not constitute problems.[19] As for the *künstlerische Probleme* that the teacher and his student repeatedly referred to, we shall leave that discussion for later.

In 1931, Sedlmayr's 'Zu einer strengen Kunstwissenschaft' (Figure 11) was generally regarded as the theoretical manifesto of the Vienna School of Art History.[20] His ideal art history consisted of two components – what he called the first and second *Kunstwissenschaft*. However, Sedlmayr also reminded his readers that these two histories of art could not be strictly separated in research practice; instead, they were intertwined and mutually dependent.

[18] *Ibid.*, S. 145, 152.

[19] Edgar Wind, 'Zur Systematik der künstlerischen Probleme', S. 438.

[20] Hans Sedlmayr, 'Zu einer strengen Kunstwissenschaft', Otto Pächt (Hrg.), *Kunstwissenschaftliche Forschungen*, Vol. 1 (1931), S. 7–32; reprinted as 'Kunstgeschichte als Kunstgeschichte' in Hans Sedlmayr, *Kunst und Wahrheit*, Mittenwald: Mäander, 1978, S. 49–80; English version: 'Toward a Rigorous Study of Art', trans. Mia Fineman, in Christopher S. Wood (ed.), *The Vienna School Reader: Politics and Art Historical Method in the 1930s*, New York: Zone Books, 2000, pp. 133–179.

The distinction between the two was made merely for the convenience of discussion, to clarify the current state of confusion. The first *Kunstwissenschaft* could determine the date and place and specific attributes of artworks and, thus, reconstruct their objective forms. It could also compare and classify artworks based on their various properties, deduce genetic connections from similar attributes, and observe changes in works along temporal and geographical lines. However, the first *Kunstwissenschaft* could address only the properties that had not yet been understood as an artistic product. Sedlmayr referred to these properties as 'external' iconography, which are the meanings of pictures that would remain unchanged even if separated from their specific artistic representations. Thus, he distinguished between 'external style' and 'internal style'. Through external style, for instance, one could determine that the overall formal appearance of the Hagia Sophia resembled that of San Vitale rather than Gothic architecture. Sedlmayr maintained that 'stylistic criticism' also belonged to the first *Kunstwissenschaft*. Formal studies and investigations of external style were auxiliary considerations for the genuine *Kunstwissenschaft*. Understanding internal style, on the other hand, was the task of the second *Kunstwissenschaft*. To explain why a particular style emerged at a specific time and place, it was necessary to recognise the *Gestalt* ('configuration') or internal structure underlying the artwork. Simply classifying sensorily experienced patterns based on external formal similarities remained inadequate.[21] In comparing the two *Kunstwissenschafts*, Sedlmayr stated that:

> Although its connections to coarser realities may be artificially suspended, the second offers a true study of art, while the first, even in its highest achievements, is not really an empirical study of art but only approaches an ever elusive knowledge of artistic phenomena through a problematic series of detours (that is, through the investigation of non-artistic facts about the work of art combined with speculations about art).[22]

[21] Hans Sedlmayr, 'Toward a Rigorous Study of Art', pp. 134–7.
[22] Hans Sedlmayr, 'Toward a Rigorous Study of Art', p. 140.

HANS SEDLMAYR

ZU EINER STRENGEN KUNSTWISSENSCHAFT

Inhaltsübersicht

VORBEMERKUNG

Jeder einzelne, der heute in der Kunstwissenschaft arbeitet, hat, wenn er mit seiner besonderen Aufgabe beginnt, schon in irgendeiner Weise zu einer ganzen Reihe von Problemen Stellung genommen, auch wenn er nichts davon weiß, auch wenn seine Stellungnahme in nichts anderem besteht, als daß er das Problem übersehen oder seine eigene Lösung für selbstverständlich gehalten hat. In dieser dunklen, halb unbewußt durcheilten Zone vor der „eigentlichen" und geschätzten Arbeit entscheidet es sich, welche Bedeutung seine Bemühungen für die sich bildende Wissenschaft haben werden, ja ob das, was er treiben wird, überhaupt noch Kunstwissenschaft ist. Man könnte die typischen „Richtungen" der bestehenden Kunstwissenschaft geradezu daraus ableiten, wie sie die einzelnen Grundprobleme lösen oder verfehlen, und eine Arbeitsgruppe, die das Bedürfnis fühlt, möglichst genau zu bezeichnen, was sie versuchen will, könnte das nicht einfacher tun, als indem sie angibt, wie sie sich zu jenen Grundfragen stellt, um die keine Kunstwissenschaft herumkommen kann.

Auch in dem folgenden Versuch wird von solchen Grundproblemen die Rede sein. Der Antitheoretiker, dem die Beschäftigung mit ihnen als fruchtloses „Theoretisieren" erscheint, übersieht, daß auch er, in unartikulierter Weise, theoretisiert, und daß von seiner unausgesprochenen Theorie auch noch die materiellen „Ergebnisse" abhängen, zu denen er gelangt[1].

[1] Siehe „Kritische Berichte" 1927—28, S. 38.

7

Figure 11. 'Zu einer strengen Kunstwissenschaft' by Sedlmayr (1931)

In essence, the first *Kunstwissenschaft* always studied on the periphery; the second *Kunstwissenschaft* truly studied art. The first served the second, and in cases where the external similarities aligned with the internal ones, the first *Kunstwissenschaft* could achieve the same results as the second. Otherwise, it relied on the second *Kunstwissenschaft*. Surveying the state of art history research of his time, Sedlmayr observed that, in terms of both the quantity of scholarly achievements and the number of active scholars, the first *Kunstwissenschaft* dominated. However, the thought that even those without an understanding of art could study the first *Kunstwissenschaft* led Sedlmayr to worry about the independence of the discipline to which he had devoted himself. As a result, he urgently declared, 'Our most urgent task is to build up the "second" study of art.'[23]

The above briefly introduced the anxieties of several representative third-generation *Kunstwissenschaftlers* regarding the state of art history in their time. It is clear that they all distrusted art research systems that had been established through empirical approaches. Panofsky's *sinnliche Eigenschaften*, Wind's *Erscheinung*, and Sedlmayr's *äußeren Stil* all pointed to properties that could be determined through external sensory experience. Sedlmayr referred to this stage of work as 'external iconography', while Wind introduced the concept of *vorkünstlerische Aufgabe* ('pre-artistic task'), which aimed to reconstruct pre-artistic facts, for example, the materials, scales, colours and subjects of paintings. However, these elements still did not involve form (not referring to *Erscheinung*). *Künstlerische Probleme*, on the other hand, could not be reconstructed, because they did not reflect any empirical facts. The former provides external points of comparison, while the latter requires interpretation, representing an *immanent-künstlerischer Ursprung* ('imminent artistic origin').[24] Those familiar with Panofsky's theory of iconology would immediately think of the pre-iconographic stages, which deals with empirically related content. The iconology stage, which seeks the 'intrinsic meaning', essentially echoes his earlier theoretical pursuits that transcended empirical approaches.[25]

[23] Hans Sedlmayr, 'Toward a Rigorous Study of Art', p. 144.

[24] Edgar Wind, 'Zur Systematik der künstlerischen Probleme', S. 439.

[25] Katharina Lorenz and Jaś Elsner expressed a similar view in the 'Translator's Introduction' to the English translation of 'Über das Verhältnis der Kunstgeschichte zur Kunsttheorie': 'the concern with meaning and with working stylistic art history into a larger picture that includes not only iconography but also the problematic of pictorial signification presages the major concerns of Panofsky's later work and especially the promulgation of "iconology"' (*'On the Relationship of Art History and Art Theory: Towards the Possibility of a Fundamental System of Concepts for a Science of Art', Critical Inquiry, Vol. 35, No. 1 (Autumn 2008)*, p. 38). For further discussion, see Fan Baiding, "Some Theoretical Sources of Iconology Studies", in *World 3: Open Iconology*, Beijing: China National Photographic Art Publishing House, 2017. pp. 150–169.

3. *Künstlerische Probleme* and Transcendental Categories

Since previous art history research still failed to get to the heart of the matter, what was the core question of *Kunstwissenschaft*, and how should we address it? Panofsky attributed the solution to *künstlerische Probleme* to internal rather than to external factors. He presented art problems as always appearing as antitheses such as *Longitudinaltendenz* ('longitudinal tendency') and *Zentralisierungstendenz* ('centralising tendency'); *Säule* ('column') and *Wand* ('wall'); and *Einzelfigur* ('individual figure') and *Gesamtaufbau* ('overall composition'). All artworks achieved an *Ausgleich* ('equilibrium') between these pairs, with each conciliation being self-contained and independent of empirical reality. Ultimately, all artistic problems implicitly pointed to a single *Urproblem* ('ur-problem'), which manifested as the opposition between *Fülle* ('volume') and *Form* ('form'). Panofsky regarded this problem as an inevitable result of the conditions for all artistic creation and, thus, he asserted that the *Urproblem* of art existed on an a priori level.[26] When this *Urproblem* sought to guide the empirical level from its a priori position, Panofsky further distinguished three pairs of contrasts within the phenomenal, especially the visual sphere: elementary values (optical versus haptic), figural values (depth versus surface), and compositional values (fusing versus splitting) (Figure 12).[27]

Before proceeding with further analysis, we should briefly address the terminology of 'transcendental' or 'a priori'. These terms likely carry distinct meanings in philosophy; however, in his own writings, Panofsky used terms such as *metempirisch*, *a priori*, and *transzendental*, often without making strict distinctions among them. For instance, at the beginning of '*On the Relationship of Art History and Art Theory*', he explained *Kunstwollen* as a *metempirischer Gegenstand* ('metempirical subject'). Yet, in *Der Begriff des Kunstwollens* (1920), he stated that the process by which *Kunstwollen* reveals the intrinsic meaning of work occurs in a *transzendental-philosophischer Bedeutung* ('transcendental-philosophical sense'). Therefore, we might

[26] The term *Fülle* was translated by the English translators Lorenz and Elsner as 'volume'. They also noted in the commentary that *Fülle* carried the additional meaning of 'richness', though they emphasised the sense of 'volume'.

[27] Erwin Panofsky, 'Über das Verhältnis der Kunstgeschichte zur Kunsttheorie', S. 130–32.

understand it this way: Panofsky used *transzendental* to refer to something beyond empirical experience; and when he used the term *a priori*, he implied a similar meaning.

Panofsky viewed his three sets of contrasts as fundamental concepts of *Kunstwissenschaft*. Their aim was not to establish a universal formula to define the stylistic characteristics of an artwork or an artistic period, but rather to explain how various *künstlerische Probleme* came into being; that is, to identify the basis on which descriptive discourse is constructed. Therefore, we should not equate Panofsky's three pairs of concepts with Wölfflin's five pairs. Unlike Wölfflin's system, Panofsky's fundamental concepts are not directly employed to interpret empirical artistic phenomena. Instead, they indicate the opposition between two principles beyond the world of appearances, from which the three pairs can generate a wide range of concepts directly addressing the empirical world, for example, linear and painterly. Like a deity atop Mount Ida, Panofsky oversees the mortal realm, while Wölfflin and his followers wrestle with the complex and diverse artistic phenomena under Panofsky's guidance. The fundamental concepts merely articulate antitheses within the domain of values beyond the phenomenal world, manifesting in variations in concrete works. They form not solutions but, rather, frameworks for artistic problems. In Panofsky's words, 'The fundamental concepts…their duty is rather, if I may repeat myself, to offer an a priori legitimated catalyst from which a discussion of the manifestations may be constructed.'[28]

This a priori theory had been in gestation for a considerable time. In his article published five years earlier interpreting Riegl's *Kunstwollen*, Panofsky had already foreshadowed his later core ideas. First, he denied that *Kunstwollen* was a psychological reality or a synthesis of artistic intentions from a particular period, arguing instead that a summation derived from the art features of a period would lead only to a phenomenological classification of stylistic characteristics without revealing the fundamental principles of style. *Kunstwollen*, on the other hand, should, he argued, be understood as a concept that could be directly derived from every artistic phenomenon. It was capable of revealing, at a fundamental level, the immanent meaning

[28] Erwin Panofsky, 'On the Relationship of Art History and Art Theory', pp. 52–53.

132 ERWIN PANOFSKY.

Auseinandersetzung zwischen »Zeit« und »Raum«; und nur aus diesem Korrelationsverhältnis wird begreiflich, daß auf der einen Seite »Fülle« und »Form« miteinander in lebendige Wechselwirkung treten, und daß auf der anderen Seite »Zeit« und »Raum« in einem individuell anschaulichen Gebilde sich vereinigen können.

Diese doppelte Problematik (die in Wirklichkeit nur den zwiefachen Aspekt einer einzigen darstellt) beherrscht, wie gesagt, das künstlerische Schaffen überhaupt, d. h. ohne Rücksicht darauf, ob es sein sinnliches Material der visuellen oder der akustischen »Anschauung« entnimmt. Unter den besonderen Bedingungen der visuellen Anschauung, d. h. unter denjenigen Bedingungen, die für die bildende Kunst, das »Kunstgewerbe« und die Architektur verbindlich sind, muß sich die genannte Problematik naturgemäß in spezifischeren Gegensätzen ausdrücken, und diese spezifisch visuellen Gegensätze, oder, genauer gesagt, diese Gegensätze spezifisch visueller Werte nun sind es, die wir als die Grundprobleme des bildnerischen und architektonischen Schaffens bezeichnen dürfen, und deren begriffliche Formulierungen daher als »Grundbegriffe der Kunstwissenschaft« zu gelten haben.

Die nachfolgende Tafel möge das Gesagte verdeutlichen.

Allgemeine Antithetik innerhalb der ontologischen Sphäre:	Spezifische Gegensätze innerhalb der phänomenalen, und zwar visuellen Sphäre:			Allgemeine Antithetik innerhalb der methodologischen Sphäre
	1. Gegensatz der Elementarwerte	2. Gegensatz der Figurationswerte	3. Gegensatz der Kompositionswerte	
Die »Fülle« steht gegenüber der »Form«	Die »optischen« Werte (Freiraum) stehen gegenüber den »haptischen« Werten (Körper)	Die »Tiefenwerte« stehen gegenüber den »Flächenwerten«	Die »Werte des Ineinander« (Verschmelzung) stehen gegenüber den »Werten des Nebeneinander« (Zerteilung)	Die »Zeit« steht gegenüber dem »Raum«

II. Es kann hier natürlich nicht der Versuch gemacht werden, diese Tafel der künstlerischen Grundprobleme, die nach dem vorigen zugleich eine Tafel der kunstwissenschaftlichen Grundbegriffe ist, methodisch abzuleiten, und ihre Vollständigkeit und Brauchbarkeit darzutun. Nur um weiteren Mißverständnissen vorzubeugen, sei folgendes hinzugesetzt:

¹) Wir bedienen uns hier der Rieglschen Termini, ohne uns aber die psychologische Ableitung dieser Termini zu eigen zu machen.

Figure 12. A diagram depicting *kunstwissenschaftliches Begriffssystem* for *Kunstwissenschaft* in Panofsky's *Zeitschrift für Ästhetik und allgemeine Kunstwissenschaft*

of a work of art and the actual root of its essence; and this process occurred in the sense of transcendental philosophy.[29] At this point, Panofsky had already recognised that, from an epistemological perspective, *Kunstwollen* could indicate the immanent meaning of an artwork, but that required the establishment of a priori category. However, Panofsky had not yet proposed

[29] Erwin Panofsky, 'Der Begriff des Kunstwollens', S. 329–31.

his categories at this time, though he did mention Riegl's concept of 'optical/tactile' and pointed out that such concepts aimed to reveal the intrinsic meanings within art phenomena.[30]

In this regard, from his understanding of the development of *Kunstwollen* to the establishment of the *kunstwissenschaftliches Begriffssystem* ('conceptual system in *Kunstwissenschaft*'), Panofsky maintained the coherence of his academic thought. Initially, he interpreted *Kunstwollen* as the intrinsic meaning hidden within art phenomena. Later, he introduced the *Urproblem* of antithesis between *Fülle* ('volume') and *Form* ('form'), from which *kunstwissenschaftliches Begriffssystem* was derived as a seemingly operational approach to understanding the intrinsic meaning, while consistently reminding us of the transcendental nature of this approach.[31] However, Panofsky did not simply emphasise the transcendental while devaluing the empirical. Instead, he believed that only through their interaction and unification could the ultimate goal of *Kunstwissenschaft* – determining *Kunstwollen* – be achieved. The conceptual system of art theory had to originate from the empirical observations provided by art history to become a tool for scientific understanding. Likewise, the findings contributed by art history could form genuine scientific knowledge only when connected to *künstlerische Probleme* formulated by art theory.[32] To this point, we are reminded of Sedlmayr's discussion of the relationship between the first and second *Kunstwissenschafts*.

When mentioning the antithesis between *Fülle* and *Form*, Panofsky explicitly acknowledged that this pair of concepts owed much to his student and friend Edgar Wind. Wind also emphasised the importance of *künstlerische Probleme* in the study of art history. His concept of 'artistic problems' essentially corresponded to Panofsky's *Urproblem*, as they did

[30] *Ibid.*, S. 334.

[31] The transcendental characteristics in Panofsky's theoretical system were influenced primarily by Kant. Many scholars have written on this topic. See Michael Podro, *The Critical Historians of Art*, New Haven and London: Yale University Press, 1982; Michael Ann Holly, *Panofsky and the Foundations of Art History*, Ithaca and London: Cornell University Press, 1984; Silvia Ferretti, *Cassirer, Panofsky, and Warburg: Symbol, Art and History*, New Haven and London: Yale University Press, 1989; Allister Neher, '"The Concept of Kunstwollen", Neo-Kantianism, and Erwin Panofsky's Early Art Theoretical Essays', *Word & Image*, Vol. 20, No.1 (2004).

[32] Erwin Panofsky, 'Über das Verhältnis der Kunstgeschichte zur Kunsttheorie', S. 144.

not reflect any empirical conditions. Unlike pre-artistic tasks, which merely provided external points of comparison (such as colour, motifs and techniques – elements that could be derived directly from the artwork), artistic problems invited interpretation and revealed the immanent-artistic origin. Wind also believed that art phenomena contained a conciliation of conflicting opposites that were determined by underlying basic thought processes. Thus, artistic problems were essentially the questions that the thought processes of *Kunstwissenschaft* posed to artistic creation. They were not questions that preceded the solutions but, rather, the premises used to interpret them. Therefore, artistic problems do not help us directly explain art phenomena, but only by conceiving artistic problems can we determine the approach needed to interpret the phenomena.[33] In this regard, Panofsky and Wind reached an epistemological consensus.

Wind also placed polar opposites in a transcendental context when discussing them. He described them as purely intellectual ideas and as the goal of *spekulative Reflexion* ('speculative reflection').[34] To interpret the external appearance of artworks, empirical reconstruction proved ineffective; one had to transcend art phenomena, and only *spekulative Reflexion* could guide us in deriving *künstlerische Probleme*.[35] To specifically illustrate the nature of antitheses in art problems, Wind took Riegl's concepts of 'subjectivistic' and 'objectivistic' as an example. He observed that Riegl, whether dealing with architecture or visual arts, could always identify *latente Gegensatze* ('latent contradiction') that conflicted with existing conditions, and that he sought to achieve a *Versöhnung* ('conciliation'). He wanted his readers to understand that the conflicts in artworks were not externally visible stylistic forms but, rather, a driven force hidden behind them. Panofsky perceived in artworks a balance between two poles, describing a completed stable state, while Wind's opposites were full of movements, suggesting an underlying force driving ebbs and flows between the poles. In this regard, Wind differed from Panofsky – a difference that aligned with their separate interpretations

33 Edgar Wind, 'Zur Systematik der künstlerischen Probleme, S. 440–41.

34 Wind stated that in Panofsky's works was seen, for the first time, a call for speculative reflection and an explanation of this method.

35 Edgar Wind, 'Zur Systematik der künstlerischen Probleme', S. 441, 446–7.

of *Kunstwollen*. Sedlmayr noted that Panofsky interpreted *Kunstwollen* as the intrinsic, objective meaning within art phenomena, thus losing the dynamic character; however, he praised Wind for correctly viewing *Kunstwollen* as a real force.[36] The latent contrasts within artworks formed an *Abfolge* ('sequence') of evolving artistic problems through continual conflictions and reconciliations, allowing Wind to see that Riegl aimed to interpret not only appearances but also internal development in art.[37] Since Wölfflin's concepts relied entirely on factors manifested as the external appearance of art, rather than logic derived from the sequence of problems, Wind pointed out that his research model, which was based on psychological laws, failed to account for such development. In other words, Wölfflin's concepts addressed only the final solutions that had taken shape, rather than the problems that gave rise to them.

After demonstrating the autonomy and transcendental nature of *künstlerische Probleme*, Wind, like Panofsky, established a system of paired concepts. However, his system was more comprehensive than Panofsky's, which consisted of only three pairs of differentiated concepts. Wind's nine pairs of concepts were divided into three groups. The first group, *Die Sphäre der qualitativen Erscheinung* ('the sphere of qualitative appearance'), was essentially identical to Panofsky's three-pair system. Wind introduced two more groups – *erscheinendes Ding* ('appearing thing') and *sich äußerndes Leben* ('self-manifesting life') – containing six additional pairs of concepts. Why did he expand Panofsky's system? Wind explicitly stated that transcendental deduction alone was insufficient.

The two visual orders in *künstlerische Probleme* must first conflict with each other. Wind emphasised that they also had to exist on the same *Ebene* ('level') and a similar *Schicht* ('layer'). In his system, *künstlerische Probleme* not only involved opposing forms but also occurred at a specific position. Therefore, when conducting systematic deductions, one must, on the one hand, define the *kategoriale Antithese* ('categorical antithesis'), and, on the other, determine the *Regionen* ('regions') where oppositions occur. The

[36] Hans Sedlmayr, 'The Quintessence of Riegl's Thought', in Richard Woodfield (ed.), *Framing Formalism: Riegl's Work*, London: Routledge, 2001, p. 15.

[37] Edgar Wind, 'Zur Systematik der künstlerischen Probleme', S. 442–3.

Urantithese ('original antithesis') between *Fülle* and *Form* cannot be used to evaluate an artwork in terms of artistic achievement. To identify the visual qualities reflecting this original antithesis in a particular work, one must descend to the visual regions; this is the key motivation behind Wind's more comprehensive system.[38] However, one should not conclude that Wind's system combined the transcendental and the empirical. He declared that all nine pairs of concepts were based on *Gestaltungsprinzipien* ('formal principles') and phenomenological conditions rather than empirical conditions. Only the externally visible *Erscheinung* were products of the empirical world.[39] Wind's concepts can be understood as residing between the transcendental and empirical levels. They are not grounded in the empirical conditions that enable the appearance to manifest; they remain abstract formal principles.

Compared to the well-articulated *Kunstwissenschaft* frameworks established by Panofsky and Wind, the theoretical declarations from the representatives of the Vienna School did not provide clearly defined research methods. Rather, they repeatedly asserted what they regard as correct or incorrect attitudes, at most offering a set of maxims. It is no surprise that in his critique of this school, Meyer Schapiro (1904–1996) stated bluntly that Sedlmayr's articles failed to introduce the methodological logic of the second *Kunstwissenschaft*.[40] What can be determined, however, is that the second *Kunstwissenschaft* maintained the transcendental nature of art research and objectively diminished the role of empirical facts within the *Kunstwissenschaft* system, even though Sedlmayr emphasised the indispensability of the first *Kunstwissenschaft*. In fact, Wind had already used the term 'structure' to refer to the immanent-artistic origin.[41] Sedlmayr claimed that the second *Kunstwissenschaft* was concerned only with the nature and internal structure of artworks to understand the internal forces that had led to their creation and formation. Thus, he emphasised that the study of individual artworks was the primary task of *Kunstwissenschaft* at that stage. Although he repeatedly reminded readers that investigating the historical context was equally

[38] Edgar Wind, 'Zur Systematik der künstlerischen Probleme', S. 458, 461.
[39] *Ibid.*, S. 471.
[40] Meyer Schapiro, 'The New Viennese School', *Art Bulletin*, Vol. 18, No. 2 (1936), p. 258.
[41] Edgar Wind, 'Zur Systematik der künstlerischen Probleme', S. 439.

important and complementary, he undoubtedly highlighted the central position of individual artworks. Moreover, he believed that the properties of individuals works can help us understand the historical events that led to their production.[42] Such insight into an artwork's internal structure could allow one to 'see' missing elements that should have been present in an artwork without physical evidence.[43] This almost metaphysical method of observation requires observing a work with an 'artistic' attitude, endowing it with artistic qualities. Otto Pächt, another key figure in this school, expressed a similar view: 'We could not apprehend an object, and indeed anything from the external world, if we did not bring to it a certain disposition, a certain attitude toward form.'[44] Following their logic, to understand artistic qualities requires a metaphysical subjective attitude, and only through this approach can the transcendent internal *Gestalt* be revealed.

By focusing on the internal qualities of individual artworks, the Vienna School was able to assert the independence of art research. It no longer needed to be entangled with other branches of the overall cultural environment. The artwork itself could form a self-contained small world. Sedlmayr was actually aware that allying with other disciplines before the discipline had established a firm foundation would risk losing its autonomy. This sense of crisis compelled them to firmly cling to a transcendental domain unaffected by any external factors.[45]

4. The Struggle of the Humanities

Almost thirty years after the publication of *Late Roman Art Industry*, Guido Kaschnitz-Weinberg (1890–1958) still referred to it as a turning point – or, perhaps, even a revolution – in the historical study of visual arts.[46] At that

[42] Hans Sedlmayr, 'Toward a Rigorous Study of Art', pp. 140, 155.

[43] Sedlmayr took Wilhelm Pinder (1878–1947) as an example, stating that Pinder had successfully understood the inner structure of the Nördlingen Altar, thereby reconstructing its missing parts. Hans Sedlmayr, 'Toward a Rigorous Study of Art', p. 140.

[44] Otto Pächt, 'The End of the Image Theory', in *The Vienna School Reader*, p. 184.

[45] Hans Sedlmayr, 'Toward a Rigorous Study of Art', pp. 155, 165–6.

[46] Guido Kaschnitz-Weinberg, 'Alois Riegl. Spätrömische Kunstindustrie. Rezension', *Gnomon*, 5, Bd., H. 4/5, April-May 1929, S. 196; English version: 'Review of Alois Riegl, *Die Spätrömische Kunstindustrie*, 1927', trans. Martin Schwarz, *Art History*, 39 (1), 2016, pp. 84–97.

time, the introduction of *Kunstwollen* not only helped *Kunstwissenschaft* take a decisive step toward the establishment of a self-sufficient methodological, but it also became an important intellectual legacy of art history. It undoubtedly had a profound influence on the theoretical explorations of German-speaking art historians in the early twentieth century. It could even be said that the major theoretical efforts of the third generation of *Kunstwissenschaftlers* were largely driven by a critique and reconstruction of *Kunstwollen*. Beyond triggering collective discussions around *Kunstwollen* in the 1920s, it also laid the foundation for two primary 'schools' in art history during the 1930s: the structural research of the Vienna School and the iconological approach of the 'Warburg Circle'. Building upon Riegl's ideas, the former viewed historical development as a metaphysical teleology of collective subjectivity and productive collective will. The latter, represented by Panofsky, presented *Kunstwollen* as an indicator for revealing intrinsic meanings, ultimately forming the third level of his iconology.

Sedlmayr criticised Panofsky's interpretation of *Kunstwollen*, while Kaschnitz was dissatisfied with Riegl's paired concepts. In essence, their critiques targeted Panofsky's approach of seeking a transcendental philosophical foundation for the discipline of art history. Kaschnitz doubted transcendental concepts due to concerns about their inadequacy in explaining historical changes.[47] Ironically, Meyer Schapiro's critique of the Vienna Circle was precisely that 'this school lacks a sufficiently historical concept to guide its scientific and rigorous historical interpretations.... [T]hey prefer teleological deductions over empirical research into historical conditions and facts.'[48] Even Otto Pächt acknowledged this weakness of his school: 'according to the usual view, history should, if possible, concern itself with the unique, here the charge of a priori construction, of ahistorical, threatens.'[49] Due to their focus on internal structures beneath appearances and deliberate emphasis on the self-sufficiency of artistic phenomena, members of the Vienna School,

[47] Martin Schwarz and Jaś Elsner, 'The Genesis of *Struktur*: Kaschnitz-Weinberg's Review of Riegl and the New Viennese School', *Art History*, 39 (1), 2016, pp. 72, 75–6.
[48] Meyer Schapiro, 'The New Viennese School', p. 260.
[49] Otto Pächt, 'The End of the Image Theory', p. 183.

despite their efforts to demonstrate their attention to historical issues, could not escape criticism for being detached from reality. Thus, even though Kaschnitz opposed Panofsky's transcendental concepts, he also acknowledged art as a direct source for understanding worldviews and *Kunstwollen* as the foundation for studying intrinsic meanings within art history. This ambivalent attitude, in turn, highlighted the Vienna School's persistence in the transcendental aspirations.[50] On one side was the historical context constraining specific artworks, and on the other was the pursuit of universal theories to ensure the autonomy of the discipline. Even Panofsky, who was criticised for his transcendental approach, advocated for balancing both in his 'Über das Verhältnis der Kunstgeschichte zur Kunsttheorie', believing that only through this balance could interpretive art history progress. However, ultimately, he placed the ontology of art above history.[51]

The transcendental framework advocated by Panofsky and Wind was not only used to address *künstlerische Probleme* within the discipline of art history but was also believed to apply to other humanities disciplines. Wind implicitly suggested that his nine pairs of concepts dealt only with the category of visual appearances, yet he believed that the appearances of other art forms could be analysed in the same way as visual arts.[52] Panofsky, however, was far more ambitious. Beyond drawing analogies between the intrinsic meanings of visual art and those found in music, poetry and other phenomena, he went so far as to assert that *Kunstwissenschaft* was connected to all humanities disciplines. Furthermore, he claimed that within a particular culture, all intellectual problems could be resolved in one and the same sense.[53]

[50] Guido Kaschnitz-Weinberg, 'Alois Riegl. Spätrömische Kunstindustrie. Rezension', S. 209–10.

[51] 'It would be comfortable and certainly spare all methodological discussion from the start if art theory and art history really had nothing in common. Alas, in truth they rely on each other reciprocally; and this reciprocity is not a coincidence but the necessary result of the fact that the work of art – like all productions of the creative mind – has the double characteristic of being determined by temporal and spatial circumstances on the one hand and on the other of forming a solution, conceptually timeless and absolute, of a priori constituted problems – of generating itself in the flow of historical making and yet reaching into the sphere of hyperhistorical validity' Erwin Panofsky, '*On the Relationship of Art History and Art Theory*', p. 67.

[52] Edgar Wind, 'Zur Systematik der künstlerischen Probleme', S. 471.

[53] Erwin Panofsky, 'Über das Verhältnis der Kunstgeschichte zur Kunsttheorie', S. 155.

In fact, the third generation of *Kunstwissenschaftlers* passionately defended the uniqueness of their discipline, seeking solutions in a realm that transcended empirical reality. This, in turn, reflected the broader struggle of the humanities against the dominance of the natural sciences. Perhaps it was the flourishing of natural sciences in the nineteenth century and their methodological support to many humanities disciplines, including art history (mainly in empirical research), that caused humanities scholars to feel both grateful for and uneasy about this dependence. Ernst Cassirer (1874–1945), Panofsky's colleague at the University of Hamburg and a crucial influence on his academic thought. His *Zur Logik der Kulturwissenschaften* (1942) reflected in many ways the intellectual trends in *Kunstwissenschaft* before the Second World War.[54] He mentioned the expression of Wilhelm von Humboldt (1767–1835), that 'language is a function and not an affection', to argue that the object of humanities research should not be limited to phenomena but should also focus on the intellectual activities of the humans that generated those phenomena.[55] In other words, the true subject of the humanities was not tangible things but, rather, the human mental activities that generated them. Following the similiar logic, *Kunstwissenschaftlers* believed that art history presented results of subjective thought acting upon materials, thus requiring interpretive principles to understand artistic phenomena through consciousness that penetrated the realm of empirical existence.[56] As Ludwig Coellen (1875–1945) remarked in a book on the methodology of art history published in the 1920s: 'the work of art is just a "dead" product, deposited by a creative intellectual process.... Art history, if it is to be a science, has to construct an explanation of the appearance of work of art, based on its origins.'[57] Thus, Cassirer argued, as in

[54] Enst Cassirer, *Zur Logik der Kulturwissenschaften: Fünf Studien*, Göteborg: Elanders boktryckeri aktiebolag, 1942. In fact, other terms, such as *Geistewissenschaft*, *Geschichtswissenschaft* and *Humanwissenschaft*, were all used at different periods to refer to the humanities in contrast to *Naturwissenschaft* (natural sciences). The two English translations – *The Logic of the Humanities* (New Haven and London: Yale University Press, 1961) and *The Logic of the Cultural Sciences* (New Haven and London: Yale University Press, 2000) – reflect this uncertainty in translating these terms.

[55] Ernst Cassirer, *The Logic of the Cultural Science*, trans. S. G. Lofts, New Haven and London: Yale University Press, p. 14.

[56] Erwin Panofsky, 'Der Begriff des Kunstwollens', S. 322.

[57] Ludwig Coellen, Über die *Methode der Kunstgeschichte: eine geschichtsphilosophische Untersuchung*, Darmstadt: Arkadenverlag, 1924; quoted from Hans Sedlmayr, 'The Quintessence of Riegl's Thought', p. 14.

Humboldt's linguistics, the most important task is to explore pure structural issues of language from inner form of language, which are independent of and unaffected by history. He believed that the same applied to *Kunstwissenschaft* and that every humanities discipline could develop its specific formal and stylistic concepts. If art history were merely a description of what had already occurred, the discipline could not develop. Taking Wölfflin as an example, he argued that Wölfflin's basic concepts, like Humboldt's, were not 'idiographic' concepts derived from 'perceptual historical material'; instead, they were aimed at establishing universal principles. He believed that Wölfflin clearly demonstrated the pure structural concepts of *Kunstwissenschaft*, thereby advancing toward universal questions.[58] Of course, Panofsky would not have agreed with Cassirer's praise of Wölfflin. However, what Panofsky opposed was not the achievements described by Cassirer but, rather, the choice.

Cassirer attempted to weaken the tendency towards a rationalist culture brought by natural sciences by emphasising the supreme status of human mental activities in the humanities. The empirical methods of natural sciences in the study of the tangible world were deemed inadequate for guiding the study of anthropomorphised cultural phenomena. After benefiting from the advancements of natural sciences, *Kunstwissenschaftlers* began to establish a unique awareness of artistic phenomena. The emergence of *Kunstwollen* led to decades of art theory being tinged with a tone of animism. Schapiro claimed he met with 'spiritualistic conceptions and with allusions to qualities or causes that we have no means of verifying' in the writings of the New Viennese School.[59] From relying initially on the methods and attitudes of natural sciences to study artworks – giving art history scientific features – to ultimately striving to get rid of the constraints of other disciplines and advocating for the purity of research objects and methods, *Kunstwissenschaft* played out an Oedipal myth in its journey from the empirical to the transcendental. With the end of the Second World War, as German-speaking art historians emigrated to America, the teleological approach to art history based on collective consciousness also collapsed. Today, the term

[58] Ernst Cassirer, *The Logic of the Cultural Science*, pp. 58-62.

[59] Meyer Schapiro, 'The New Viennese School', p. 459.

Kunstwissenschaft still appears in German writings, but its meaning has long diverged from its original connotations. Jan Białostocki (1921–1988) once optimistically declared Panofsky's 'Über das Verhältnis der Kunstgeschichte zur Kunsttheorie' to be 'Prolegomena to any future art history which could claim to be a science'.[60] Unfortunately, at least so far, the vision of the third generation of *Kunstwissenschaftlers* has been neither theoretically extended nor widely applied in practice.

[60] Jan Białostocki, 'Erwin Panofsky (1892-1968): Thinker, Historian, Human Being', *Simiolus*, Vol. 4, No. 2 (1970), p. 73.

III

KULTURWISSENSCHAFT AND *KUNSTWISSENSCHAFT*

1. Warburg and his Journey to Indian Territory

For enthusiasts of art history, if they have heard of the term *Kulturwissenschaft* ('cultural science'), it is most likely due to Aby Warburg's private library – the Kulturwissenschaftliche Bibliothek Warburg. Most of the time, he is regarded as an art historian. His distinctive research approach, along with the circle of scholars formed around his library, made outstanding contributions to the development of many humanities disciplines, including *Kunstwissenschaft*. However, Warburg preferred to observe human cultural survival under the name of *Kulturwissenschaft*, with visual art as his primary entry point – or, in his own words, he aimed at a *kunsthistorische Kulturwissenschaft* ('art-historical cultural science').[1] Today, many people are familiar with the encyclopedic intellectual framework of the Warburg Library that encompassed all aspects of the humanities and fostered numerous interdisciplinary classic works. At certain moments in history, the term *Kulturwissenschaft* was synonymous with the humanities.[2] This raises the question: During the formative period of modern art history, namely from the nineteenth to the early twentieth century, what exactly was the relationship between Warburg's concept of *Kulturwissenschaft* and *Kunstwissenschaft*? How should we understand their theoretical significance in the broader academic context at that time? Warburg's journey to visit Indian tribes in America may be an appropriate starting point for answering these questions.

In September 1895, Warburg travelled to the United States to attend the 1 October wedding of his brother, Paul, to Nina Loeb; the following year,

[1] WIA III. 113. 6 'Über die Methode einer kunstgeschichtlichen Kulturwissenschaft', quoted from Katia Mazzucco, 'Images on the Move: Some Notes on the Bibliothek Warburg Bildersammlung (Hamburg) and the Warburg Institute Photographic Collection (London)', *Art Libraries*, Vol. 38, No. 4 (2013), p. 23.

[2] Ernst Cassirer published *The Logic of Cultural Sciences* in his later years, which actually addressed the humanities as a whole.

he visited the Pueblo regions in Arizona and New Mexico (Figure 13).[3] In 1923, at the Heilanstalt Bellevue in Kreuzlingen, Switzerland, he delivered a lecture in German that later became known as the *Schlangenritual* ('serpent ritual'), a study based on the research he had conducted during this earlier exploration of Indigenous tribes.[4] Gombrich stated in his biography of Warburg that 'More has been published in English on this episode in

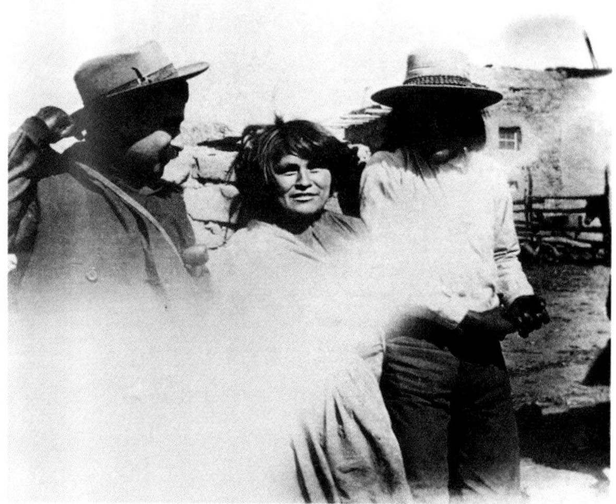

Figure 13. Warburg (left) with a Zuñi girl and Pueblo man, New Mexico, April 1896

[3] Davide Stimilli, 'Aby Warburg in America again', *RES: Anthropology and Aesthetics*, No. 48 (Autumn, 2005), p. 193. This marriage strengthened the business connections between the Warburg family and the Loeb family. Nina Loeb's brother James Loeb (1867–1933) later established the famous Loeb Classical Library project. Regarding details of Warburg's journey amongst the Indian tribes of North America, we can refer to Claudia Naber, 'Pompeji in Neu-Mexico: Aby Warburgs amerikanische Reise', *Freibeuter*, 38 (1988), p. 89; and Uwe Fleckner (Hrg.), *Aby Warburg, Bilder aus dem Gebiet der Pueblo-Indianer in Nord-Amerika: Vorträge und Fotografien*, Band III.2 in *Gesammelte Schriften*, Berlin: de Gruyter, 2018.

[4] The English version of this lecture was first published as 'A Lecture on Schlangenritual' in the *Journal of the Warburg Institute*, Vol. 2 (April 1939), pp. 277–92. Later, Ulrich Raulff compiled *Schlangenritual: Ein Reisebericht* (Berlin: Wagenbach, 1988) based on Warburg's manuscripts held at the Warburg Institute, which is currently considered the definitive version, including Raulff's 'Nachwort'. Based on this version, Michael P. Steinberg translated *Images from the Region of the Pueblo Indians of North America* (Ithaca: Cornell University Press, 1995). Philippe-Alain Michaud included Warburg's notes for the Kreuzlingen lecture on the serpent ritual in an appendix to *Aby Warburg and the Image in Motion*, trans. Sophie Hawkes (New York: Zone Books, 2004, pp. 293–335). For Warburg's diaries from this period, we can refer to *Photographs at the Frontier: Aby Warburg in America 1895-1896*, Benedetta Cestelli Guidi and Nicholas Mann (eds.), London: The Warburg Institute, 1998.

Warburg's life than on any other aspect of his work...and Warburg's own lecture about his experience among the Indians is the only one of his writings which is available in English'.[5]

Today, more and more of Warburg's works have been translated into English, and research on his works has become a prominent academic field. His journey to America remains the topic scholars are most interested in. Many of them connect the work of this art historian with anthropological studies, a connection first made by Warburg's assistant, Fritz Saxl (1890–1948), who wrote an article specifically about Warburg and his visit to New Mexico.[6] He first affirmed that Warburg's work primarily addressed problems of art history, but he emphasised that Warburg was not merely immersed in archives nor was he entirely preoccupied with the art history of Florence. Instead, he focused on a relatively short period of the last decades of the fifteenth century – the so-called early Renaissance – which Warburg considered significant for human history. In a departure from Johann Winckelmann's (1717–1768) attitude to the 'noble' classical in the eighteenth century, Warburg wanted to uncover what 'antiquity' meant to the Italians of the fifteenth century. During his university years, Warburg was introduced to the study of religious mythology through Hermann Usener (1834–1905), a scholar who – like James Frazer in Britain [1854–1941], sought to understand the classical texts and the origins of Greco-Roman religions through the surviving remnants of pagan culture. Warburg, for his part, drew inspriartion from the Pueblo Indians in two aspects for addressing problems related to the European classical antiquity: first, Indian rituals were expressions of religious passion; secondly, he observed various modes of creating and transmitting symbols. Within this context, Saxl argued that

[5] E.H. Gombrich, *Aby Warburg*, p. 90.

[6] Fritz Saxl, 'Warburg's Visit to New Mexico', in *Lectures*, London: Warburg Institute, 1957, pp. 325–30. Gombrich discovered that Warburg was enlightened from the ideas of anthropologist Adolf Bastian (1826–1905), see E.H. Gombrich, *Aby Warburg*, pp. 285–7; see more in Ulrich Raulff, 'Nachwort', in *Schlangenritual*, S. 73–5; Roland Kany, *Mnemosyne als Programm. Geschichte, Erinnerung und die Andacht zum Unbedeutenden im Werk von Usener, Warburg und Benjamin*, Tübingen: Niemeyer, 1987; Maria Michela Sassi, 'Dalla Scienza delle Religioni di Usener ad Aby Warburg', in *Aspetti di Hermann Usener Filologo della Religione*, Pisa: Giardini, 1982, pp. 65–91; Claude Imbert, 'Aby Warburg, Between Kant and Boas: From Aesthetics to the Anthropology of Images', *Qui Parle*, Vol. 16, No. 1 (Summer 2006), pp. 1–45; Peter Burke, 'History and Anthropology in 1900', in *Photographs at the Frontier*, pp. 20–27.

'it was not the least of his merits that he [Warburg] turned to American anthropology for help in solving it.'[7]

In the early twentieth century, anthropologist Bronisław Malinowski (1884–1942) remarked in a lecture on mythology that 'I believe that the study of mythology as it functions and works in primitive societies should anticipate the conclusions drawn from the material of higher civilizations. Some of this material has come down to us only in isolated literary texts, without its setting in actual life, without its social context, Such is the mythology of the ancient classical peoples and of the dead civilizations of the Orient. In the study of myths, classical scholars should consult anthropologists."[8] In this light, Warburg was merely one of many practitioners of his time. Before visiting the Indigenous tribes of America, Warburg discovered the Smithsonian Institution while in Washington, D.C., where he became aware of the pioneering ethnological protagonists Frank Cushing (1857–1900) and James Mooney (1861–1921); in New York, he also knew Franz Boas (1858–1942) (Figure 14).[9] Although Warburg had consciously engaged with anthropological knowledge and maintained a correspondence with Boas, some scholars remain sceptical about the connection between his research and anthropology.[10] In an anthology exploring the relationship between art history and anthropology, David Freedberg bluntly pointed out that most articles discussing Warburg's visit to the Pueblo regions merely reiterated the same ideas without critical insight. He argued that these studies exaggerated Warburg's role as a pioneer linking art history and anthropology – a claim that, unfortunately, most anthropologists did not acknowledge.[11] Both Freedberg and Saxl served as directors of the Warburg Institute, but they disagreed on whether the founder's work could

[7] Fritz Saxl, 'Warburg's Visit to New Mexico', p. 326.

[8] This lecture, titled "Myth in Primitive Psychology", was delivered in 1925 at the University of Liverpool, which was published next year in the same title. The quotation here, see Bronislaw Malinowski, *Myth in Primitive Psychology*, London: Kegan Paul, Trench, Trubner & Co. Ltd, 1926, p. 122.

[9] Peter Burke, 'History and Anthropology in 1900', p. 27.

[10] Benedetta Cestelli Guidi, 'Aby Warburg and Franz Boas: Two Letters from the Warburg Archive', *RES: Anthropology and Aesthetics*, Vol. 52 (Autumn 2007), pp. 221–30. See also, Paul Taylor, "Henri Frankfort, Aby Warburg and 'Mythopoeic Thought'", Journal of Art Historiography, No. 5 (December 2011), p. 12.

[11] David Freedberg, 'Warburg's Mask: A Study in Idolatry', in Mariët Westermann (ed.), *Anthropologies of Art*, Williamstown, Massachusetts: Sterling and Francine Clark Art Institute, p. 3.

be classified as anthropology. Perhaps no other example better illustrates the difficulty of defining the disciplinary boundaries of Warburg's American journey and his lecture on *Schlangenritual*.

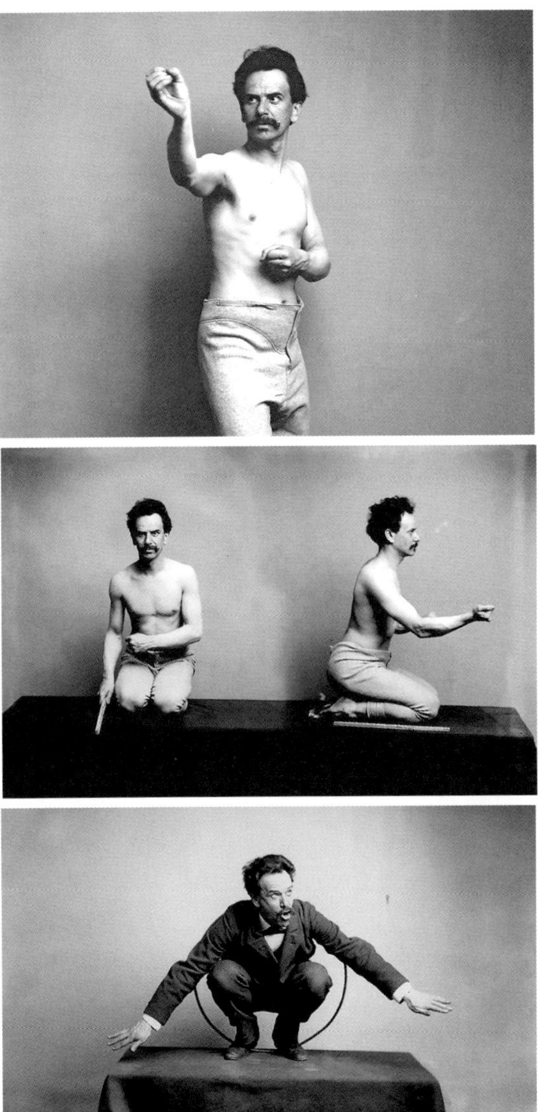

Figure 14. Franz Boas performing a Kwakiutl ritual dance

I do not aim to choose between the perspectives of the two directors nor discuss the details of Warburg's journey to New Mexico. Instead, I wish to discuss the ambiguity of Warburg's journey to Indian territory. His lecture years later at Kreuzlingen undoubtedly stands as the most unique text among all his works, offering insight into many academic motivations, and its ambiguity also reveals the connections between *Kunstwissenschaft*, *Kulturwissenschaft* and their relationships with other disciplines and theories of the nineteenth century.

Warburg's investigation of the Pueblos and their various tribal rituals partly reflected the enthusiasm of many Europeans for primitive cultures at the time. Exotic handmade artefacts became the topics of discussions; new modes of transportation emerged throughout the nineteenth century international exhibitions were held in various locations; and European powers systematically acquired objects from their colonies to establish ethnological museums. These factors fuelled an interest in Indigenous cultures and promoted related research, involving experts from ethnology, ethnography psychology and art history.[12] The prominent art historians familiar to us – such as Semper, Riegl and Josef Strzygowski (1862 – 1941) – had paid close attention to objects that cannot easily be classified as belonging to the canon of high art. This preference for the primitive origins of art and for "minor arts" can serve as point of departure, prompting us to consider *Kunstwissenschaft* and *Kulturwissenschaft* (primarily in Warburg's sense) together as an integrated whole in order to reflect on their core questions and aims. Since these two approaches have usually been explored separately, once they are placed side by side, a few questions inevitably arise: Why did *Kunstwissenschaft* become dissatisfied with traditional art history? What is the similarity and difference between *Kunstwissenschaft* and *Kulturwissenschaft*? Do they have anything in common in the methodological approaches and primary problems they seek to solve? How did they construct their respective frameworks from scientific instruments and theories, either natural or human?

[12] Ulrich Pfisterer, 'Origins and Principles of World Art History: 1900 (and 2000)', in Kitty Zijlmans and Wilfried van Damme (eds), *World Art Studies: Exploring Concepts and Approaches*, Amsterdam: Valiz, 2008, p. 70.

Faced with these questions, we would better study *Kulturwissenschaft* and *Kunstwissenschaft* within the nineteenth-century knowledge network of interconnected disciplines. Strictly speaking, they are neither distinct disciplines nor clearly defined methodologies. Each had its own objects of study and pressing problems to address. Therefore, we might describe them as two academic ideals influenced by interactions with other disciplines. In addition to the German traditions of philosophy and aesthetics, the theoretical and methodological formation of *Kulturwissenschaft* and *Kunstwissenschaft* also relied on contributions from biology, physiology, anthropology and psychology. Furthermore, we must consider how these two frameworks responded to the numerous academic trends, concepts and research approaches of the time, such as Darwin or Darwinism, evolutionary theory, positivism, neo-Kantianism, unity, temporality, *Völkerpsychologie* ('national psychology') and survivals. *Kulturwissenschaft* and *Kunstwissenschaft* were woven into a complex, multidimensional fabric along with other theories and ideas, almost all of which had originated from other fields. Although these two ideals were often discussed separately, they emerged from the same intellectual soil.

Therefore, it would be difficult to understand the emergence and development of the two ideals without considering the academic and intellectual environment of the nineteenth century. This chapter attempts to explore the core issues relating to *Kulturwissenschaft* and *Kunstwissenschaft* in the context of the broader intellectual landscape of the time, and to define their basic frameworks through their connections with other disciplines.

2. Stereotype and Psychic Unity

Today, the connection between Warburg and cultural history or *Kulturwissenschaft* has almost become accepted. He actively tied his name to this concept. Gombrich described Warburg's belief in the potential of *Kulturwissenschaft* as a 'burning faith'.[13] However, most of the time Warburg remained concerned with fundamental questions of art history – questions that his contemporaries in art history also attempted to solve within the framework of *Kunstwissenschaft*. Warburg differed from his peers essentially

13 E.H. Gombrich, *Ideals and Idols: Essays on Values in History and in Art*, Oxford: Phaidon, 1979, p. 53.

only in the approach. Therefore, in my view, any debate about whether Warburg was an art historian, cultural historian or expert in other fields is not the point. In the process of understanding and exploring knowledge, people tend to adopt specific categories or frameworks, which play crucial roles in forming knowledge systems and establishing the autonomy of disciplines. However, we should avoid becoming overly obsessed with definitions or expending excessive energy on delineating boundaries, as these boundaries are not always fixed and are in flux .In his famous article discussing the frescoes of Palazzo Schifanoia, Warburg encouraged his contemporaries to view the ancient, medieval and modern worlds as a coherent historical unity without fearing *grenzpolizeiliche Befangenheit* (border guards).[14]

In this essay on European Renaissance art is embedded a fundamental logic underlying Warburg's studies of *Schlangenritual.* Warburg chose the word *schwächer* ('weaker') to describe one of the frescoes' painters, intending to observe through this 'weakness' how classical antiquity influenced the art and culture of the early Renaissance, because the less talented painter, unlike Francesco Cossa (*c.*1430–*c.*1477), cannot resist the dry program.[15] In other words, it is easier to observe the influences these artists were subjected to, as well as their creative intentions, through their weaknesses. Wind was perhaps the first to recognise this point; he noted that Warburg had a preference for imperfect works:

> he interested himself just as much in the artistically bad picture as in the good, and indeed often more so, for a reason which he himself explicitly acknowledged – because it had more to teach him. In his study of the iconographic meaning of the cycle of frescoes in the Palazzo Schifanoia – a pictorial enigma which he solved brilliantly – he went first to the

[14] Aby Warburg, 'Italienische Kunst und internationale Astrologie im Palazzo Schifanoja zu Ferrara', Gertrud Bing (Hrg.), *Gesammelte Schriften*, Leipzig and Berlin: B. G. Teubner, 1932, Bd. 2, S. 478; For English versions, see Peter Wortsman's translation in Gert Schiff (ed.), *German Essays on Art History*, New York: The Continuum Publishing Company, 1988, pp. 234–54 and David Britt's translation in *The Renewal of Pagan Antiquity* (Los Angeles: The Getty Research Institute, 1999), pp. 563–92.

[15] '...wo die schwächere künstlerische Persönlichkeit das trockene Programm nicht durch Belebung zu überwinden vermag', Aby Warburg, 'Italienische Kunst und internationale Astrologie im Palazzo Schifanoja zu Ferrara', S. 472.

> master who seemed to him to be the weakest. And why? Because the problem posed by the task with which the artist had to wrestle was easier to see in the flaws of the undistinguished work: the complicated structure of the major work made the problem much harder to pick out, because the artist resolved it with such a display of virtuosity.[16]

Thus, a bold yet reasonable conjecture is that Warburg, perhaps with a similar attitude, chose primitive pagan humanity – based on his 'impressions' of the Pueblo Indians – as a subject within his research. In his lecture manuscripts and notes, he expressed his desire to find a parallel in the European classical tradition to examine how the paganism worldview developed – from primitive paganism beliefs, through classical antiquity, and, finally, to the modern era.[17] A similar approach can also be observed in Riegl's work. The research subjects on which Riegl focused – for example, late Roman art and early modern Dutch art – were once considered transitional or declining periods that neither excelled in aesthetic value nor belonged to any existing artistic category. However, Riegl believed that such periods, rather than those in which artworks flourished, could better reveal the essence of historical changes in art.[18]

Through the tribal vessels and the *kachina* masks, Warburg aimed to observe the history of symbolic forms (Figure 15).[19] He compared the kachina dolls to 'the figures of saints that hang in Catholic farmhouses', and further suggested that 'from the ornamental treatment of animals, one can see how this manner of seeing and thinking could lead to symbolic pictographic writing'.[20] Warburg had read Semper's works and transcribed passages from

---

[16] Edgar Wind, 'Warburg's Concept of *Kulturwissenschaft* and its Meaning for Aesthetics', p. 34.

[17] Aby Warburg, *Images from the Region of the Pueblo Indians of North America*, p. 4. However, we must distinguish between Warburg's original purpose in visiting the Indigenous tribe of America and his intentions in the *Schlangenritual* report nearly thirty years later.

[18] Michael Gubser, *Time's Visible Surface*, p. 24.

[19] Salvatore Settis, 'Kunstgeschichte als vergleichende Kulturwissenschaft: Aby Warburg, die Pueblo-Indianer und das Nachleben der Antike', in Thomas Gaethgens (Hrg.), *Künstlerischer Austausch/Artistic Exchange*, XXVIII. *Internationalen Kongresses für Kunstgeschichte Berlin 1992*, Bd. 1, Berlin: Akademie Verlag, 1993, S. 145; David Freedberg, 'Pathos a Oraibi: Ciò che Warburg non vide', in Claudia Cieri Via and Pietro Montani (eds), *Lo Sguardo di Giano. Aby Warburg fra tempo e memoria*, Turin: Nino Aragno, 2004, p. 579.

[20] Aby Warburg, *Images from the Region of the Pueblo Indians of North America*, pp. 7–8.

the writings of that veteran art historian into his notes. Some of these notes were made during his participation in August Schmarsow's (1853–1936) seminars in Florence, while others were recorded during his doctoral dissertation period. Warburg, in the early stages of forming his ideas, drew inspiration from Semper's description of the static and dynamic states of pendant ornaments: 'Just as the garment at rest was, not without reason, previously called a macrocosmic ornament, so too, in motion – fluttering in the air – it must clearly be regarded as an ornament of direction.'[21] The fabric oscillates between this periodic movement and more linear directional ornaments, evoking a particular mood, or even what might be called *Pathos*. In the appendix of his dissertation, Warburg quoted Semper: 'The aesthetics of pure beauty have their material foundation in Dynamics and Statics.'[22] We know that Warburg's essay on Botticelli discussed the representation of 'accessories in motion' in fifteenth-century painting. If we align Semper's 'aesthetics of pure beauty' with Warburg's notion of *Pathos*, then the latter must also adhere to specific matters. Thus, Warburg would search for his *Pathosformel* in the garments of ancient nymphs and the ornamentation of the artworks of the Indians.

As a primitive form of art, ornamentation captivated Warburg and many other representatives of the *Kunstwissenschaft* whose ultimate goal was to reveal the laws of artistic development through the fundamental units that constituted complex art. In the nineteenth century, since ornamentation was a focus of many academic disciplines, art history and the culture of 'primitive' humans were even written as the history of ornamentation. Until the turn of the century, many classic publications on art history dealt with ornamentation, including those of Semper, Riegl, Wilhelm Worringer (1881–1965), and Josef Strzygowski (1862–1941).[23] From the perspective of art history, this shared interest in the origins of art is what motivated

[21] Gottfried Semper, 'Über die formelle Gesetzmässigkeit des Schmuckes und dessen Dedeutung als Kunstsymbol', *Monatsschrift des wissenschaftlichen Vereins in Zürich*, Bd. 1 (1856), S.114.

[22] Aby Warburg, Dissertation Handexemplar, WIA III. 40.1.1.2, p. 10, cited in Spyros Papapetros, 'World Ornament: The Legacy of Gottfried Semper's 1856 Lecture on Adornment', *RES: Anthropology and Aesthetics*, No. 57/58 (Spring/Autumn 2010), p. 316.

[23] Marlite Halbertsma, 'The Many Beginnings and the One End of World Art History in Germany 1900-1933', in *World Art Studies: Exploring Concepts and Approaches*, pp. 92–3.

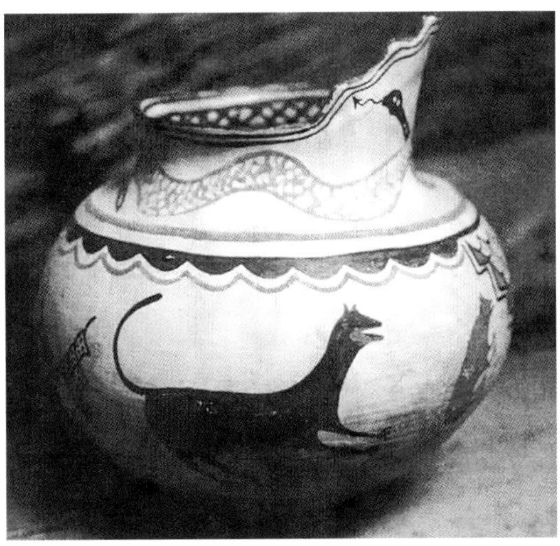

Figure 15. Pueblo vase from Aby Warburg's collection

art historians to explore primitive cultures and their artefacts. However, it should be noted that the main theoretical impetus for this phenomenon came from anthropologists and *Völkerpsychologie*; they were the first to examine primitive humans with an academic attitude, thereby providing a reasonable starting point for subsequent studies in art history. Some anthropologists, for example, Boas, went so far as to write their monographs discussing primitive art.[24]

The popular concepts at the time reflected the main concerns of anthropology: race, culture, evolution, nature, animism and irrationality. One prevailing view was that certain groups lacked culture or had lower cultural levels; they were, accordingly, seen as closer to nature. Such groups were called *Naturvölker* ('natural people'), in contrast to *Kulturvölker* ('cultured people'). Since they lacked what Europeans considered 'high culture', *Naturvölker* were regarded as occupying a lower rank of humanity, an inferior position in the framework of social evolution. Based on such theories, Europeans studied cultures worldwide, identifying cultural regions,

[24] Franz Boas, *Primitive Art*, Oslo: H. Aschehoug & Company, 1927.

investigating the psychologies of different peoples, and exploring how cultural characteristics evolved over time.[25]

In a book review of an ethnological work, Adolf Bastian (1826–1905) (Figure 16) argued that the stereotype of thought were most clearly visible in primitive cultures and, thus, that they could be used to solve the most advanced cultural problems.[26] The ideas expressed by Bastian, one of the founders of the Berlin Anthropological Society, reflected contemporary interest in *Naturvölker*.[27] *Anthropologie der Naturvölker* by Theodor Waitz (1821–1864) was described by the editor of its English edition as representing the current state of anthropological science on the European continent.[28] From *Naturvölker*, or primitive societies, anthropologists hoped to discover the essence of human nature and reflect on modern Europeans, as Waitz stated:

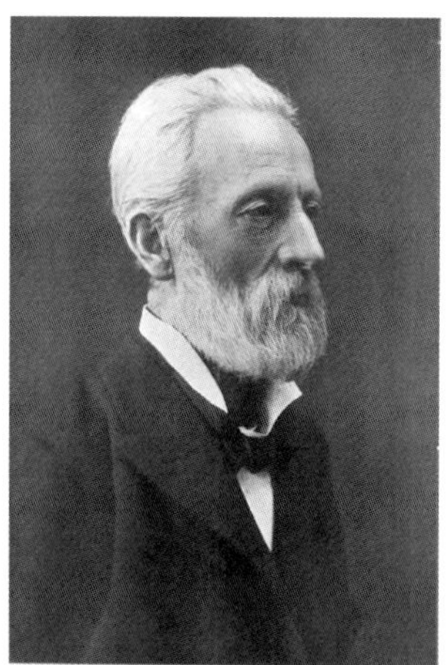

> The civilized European is accustomed to look so much down upon the so-called savage, that he deems it an insult to be compared with him; and yet, even in the midst of civilization we find the traces of customs, manners, and modes of thinking, which, like the relapse of civilized men into a savage state, prove their intimate connection.[29]

Figure 16. Adolf Bastian

[25] Peter Burke, 'History and Anthropology in 1900', p. 20.

[26] 'So wird uns auch der stereotype Gedankengang, wie er in den primitiven Naturstämmen am deutlichsten durchscheinbar ist, im methodischen Gang der Entwicklung die höchsten Culturfragen lösen, um da den Anhalt eines Naturgesetzes zu gewähren, wo bisher auf trügerisch umschleierten Gebieten...', Adolf Bastian, 'Review of *Völkerkunde* by Oscar Peschel', *Zeitschrift für Ethnologie*, 6, 1874, S. 149.

[27] Andrew Zimmerman, *Anthropology and the Place of Knowledge in Imperial Berlin*, San Diego: University of California, 1998, especially Chapter 3. This paper was later written into a monograph: *Anthropology and Antihumanism in Imperial Germany*, Chicago and London: The University of Chicago Press, 2001.

[28] J. Frederick Collingwood (ed.), *Introduction to Anthropology*, p. xiv, in Theodor Waitz, *Anthropology of Primitive Peoples*, London: The Anthropological Society, 1863.

[29] Theodor Waitz, *Anthropology of Primitive Peoples*, Vol. 1, p. 307.

According to Bastian, the essence of the nature of man is created by the unity of *Körper* ('body' or 'matter') and *Geist* ('mind'). With the progression of cultural development, human intellectual life becomes increasingly richer and more complex. The mind remains relatively independent, while the body is regulated and constrained by the environment. Examining the broad panorama of historical and geographical changes – studying groups of people at different points in time and space – reveals that the originally unified patterns of thought within the human mind become entangled in a complex maze of diverse actions and ideas. These actions and ideas, in turn, influence, stimulate and reshape one another, thereby leading to the formation of different worldviews over time. However, at their origin, all humans share a fixed Stereotype of *Geist*:

> Properly speaking, the mind and the body are one, and together make man This unity of mind and matter, created anew each moment, is the essence of the nature of man.... the same number of psychological elements (like cells of a plant) is circulating in regular and uniform rotation in the heads of all people, and that this is so for all times and places!... after removing the flesh of local and temporal variations in language and idiom, we encounter the same small number of psychological kernels.... In incidental features of narration, in nursey tales and proverbs, sayings and modes of speech, we encounter the same idea, be it in England or Abyssinia, in India or Scandinavia, in Spain or on Tahiti, in Mexico as well as in Greece.[30]

In primitive societies, the original patterns of thought are passed down through the generations like truth. Art historians studying the origins of art respond to anthropologists' investigations into the essence of human nature in primitive societies.

The exploration of various stereotypes in *Naturvölker* and, through them,

[30] Adolf Bastian, 'The Psychic Unity of Mankind and Some Elementary Symbols', in Klaus-Peter Köpping, *Adolf Bastian and the Psychic Unity of Mankind: The Foundations of Anthropology in Nineteenth Century Germany*, Münster: LIT Verlag, 2005, pp. 179–80.

the examination of higher cultures reveals an underlying belief in the spiritual consistency of humans. Bastian hypothesised that if a large-scale statistical survey could be conducted across historical and geographical boundaries, it would reveal the same number of psychological elements circulating regularly and consistently in the minds of all humans, across all times and places.[31]

Similarly, Weitz, in his *Introduction to Anthropology*, posited that psychology was the key method for studying human cultural phenomena. He maintained his belief in the uniform intellectual capacity from the Greeks to the Hottentots.[32] The opening words of Warburg's Kreuzlingen lecture echoed this idea: 'Es ist ein altes Buch zu blättern, Athen-Oraibi, alles Vettern' ('An old book tells us: Athenians and Oraibian are of the same kinship').[33] This notion has a long history. Bartolomé de las Casas (1484–1566), in his *Apologética historia de las Indias* (1552–9), compared the customs of the Mexicans to those of the inhabitants of ancient Greece and Rome. He recognised the mastery of Mexican artisans, asserting that if modern Europeans admired the ancient pagan world, there was no reason to undervalue Mexican culture.[34] Saxl had described Warburg's journey to America from 1895 to 1896 as 'a journey to the archetypes'.[35] For modern Europeans, including Warburg, both the ancient pagan civilisations and primitive cultures were equally unfamiliar in their temporal and spatial distance, hence the logical premise of this 'journey to the archetypes'.

Völkerpsychologie regards language, religion, myth and art as cultural phenomena representing collective expressions. It emphasises their importance in revealing driving forces or principles of historical development. Therefore, Bastian acknowledged that all humans shared the same psychological elements, while maintaining that external regional and temporal variations created different thought patterns.[36] In art history, although there is no direct

[31] Adolf Bastian, 'The Psychic Unity of Mankind and Some Elementary Symbols', p. 180; E.H. Gombrich, *Aby Warburg*, p. 90.

[32] Ulrich Pfisterer, 'Origins and Principles of World Art History: 1900 (and 2000)', p. 73.

[33] Aby Warburg, *Images from the Region of the Pueblo Indians of North America*, p. 1.

[34] Christopher Wood, *A History of Art History*, Princeton and Oxford: Princeton University Press, 2019, p. 73.

[35] Fritz Saxl, 'Warburg's Visit to New Mexico', p. 326.

[36] Ulrich Pfisterer, 'Origins and Principles of World Art History: 1900 (and 2000)', p. 74; Klaus-Peter Köpping, *Adolf Bastian and the Psychic Unity of Mankind*, p. 180.

evidence that Riegl read Bastian's works, Riegl's concept of *Kunstwollen* demonstrated a striking parallel to Bastian's theories. Contrary to materialist views, Riegl believed that art possessed an intrinsic vitality; he affirmed its creative self-development; and he maintained that artistic forms and concepts were transmitted from one generation to the next and from one culture to another. This resembled Bastian's description of thought patterns originating in primitive societies and being 'passed on to the next generations'.[37] All peoples worldwide and at all times possessed artistic impulses, but they differed due to external 'local and temporal variations'. In Rieg's words,

> All such human *Wollen* is directed toward self-satisfaction in relation to the surrounding environment (in the widest sense of the word, as it relates to the human being externally and internally).... man wants to interpret the world as it can most easily be done in accordance with his inner drive (which may change with nation, location and time). The character of this *Wollen* is always determined by what may be termed the conception of the world at a given time [*Weltanschauung*] (again in the widest sense of the term), not only in religion, philosophy, science, but also in government and law, where one or the other form of expression mentioned above usually dominates.[38]

As a driving force behind the art, Riegl's *Kunstwollen* is also a 'stereotype' shared by all humans, appearing in different forms at different times and places, thus creating diverse styles. Indeed, the view that art was governed by an impulsive force was discussed among scholars at the time, and Riegl undoubtedly served as its foremost advocate.[39]

To some extent, the development of *Völkerpsychologie* in the late nineteenth and early twentieth centuries prompted art historians to direct their attention beyond Europe, thus forming the foundation of modern world

[37] Alois Riegl, *Problems of Style: Foundations for a History of Ornament*, trans. Evelyn Kain, Princeton and New Jersey: Princeton University Press, 1992, p. xxvii.
[38] Alois Riegl, *Late Roman Art Industry*, p. 231.
[39] Yrjö Hirn, *The Origins of Art: A Psychological & Sociological Inquiry*, London: Macmillan & Co., 1900, Chapter 2 ('The Art-Impulse').

art studies and inspiring new perspectives on the fundamental questions of *Kunstwissenschaft*. For instance, in an article, Schmarsow attempted to systematically summarise the implications of *Völkerpsychologie* and proposed an anthropology for the emerging *Kunstwissenschaft*.[40] However, Schmarsow was inspired by Ernst Grosse (1862–1927) (Figure 17) and his work, *Die Anfänge der Kunst* (1894).[41] Although the title suggests a focus on the origins of art, the first two chapters discuss the aim and the way of *Kunstwissenschaft*. Grosse applied comparative ethnology to the study of art history and attempted to reshape *Kunstwissenschaft* into an objective and scientific discipline that aimed to uncover the regularities behind the individual phenomena. He considered that the scope of contemporary art history was excessively narrow, arguing that *Kunstwissenschaft* should expand its research to all peoples and focus especially on previously neglected groups. All forms of art should be entitled to equal consideration, in light of their inner qualities. However, Grosse believed that if we were ever to attain a true Kunstwissenschaft for civilized peoples, it would necessarily have to be preceded by an understanding of the nature and conditions of the art of 'savage' people. Thus, he began exploring *Naturvölker* and their art, hoping by so doing to reveal the laws of artistic development. His understanding of *Kunstwissenschaft* was such that it did not require the exhaustive examination of every corner of the art world – which would have been impossible to do, anyway, as the factors underlying artworks are infinite in any given context. Rather, *Kunstwissenschaft* could only hope to show the 'regular and fixed relations exist between certain forms of culture and art'.[42]

Naturvölker helped Grosse to observe the laws of art. A year before Warburg's journey to America, Grosse had already, from an art historical perspective, articulated the reasons behind Warburg's linking of Pueblo rituals with European classical culture. Although Grosse acknowledged that

[40] August Schmarsow, 'Kunstwissenschaft und Völkerpsychologie: ein Versuch zur Verständigung', *Zeitschrift für Ästhetik und allgemeine Kunstwissenschaft*, 2 (1907), S. 305–39.

[41] Ernst Grosse, *Die Anfänge der Kunst*, Freiburg: J.C.B. Mohr, 1894; English version, *The Beginnings of Art*, New York: D. Appleton and Company, 1897.

[42] Ernst Grosse, *The Beginnings of Art*, pp. 7, 8, 21.

artistic endeavours might not be entirely pure at the lowest stages of culture, his view was that they could still be observed everywhere and were essentially identical to the forms expressed in higher stages of culture. While the forms of primitive art might initially appear unfamiliar or even devoid of artistic value, upon closer examination, it became evident that they adhere to the same principles as those governing the creation of high art. A passage from Grosse effectively captures the core idea of artistic uniformity:

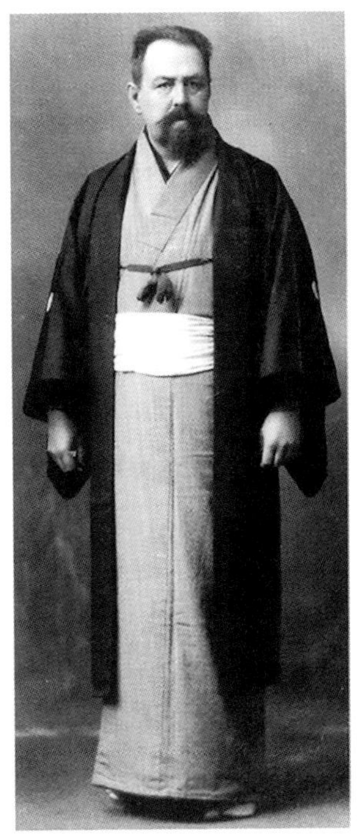

Figure 17. Ernst Grosse

> Our investigation has proved what aesthetics has hitherto only asserted: that there are, for the human race at least, generally effective conditions for aesthetic pleasure, and consequently generally valid laws of artistic creation. As against this fundamental agreement, the differences between primitive and higher art forms appear to be more of a quantitative than a qualitative sort. The emotions represented in primitive art are narrow and rude, its materials are scanty, its forms are poor and coarse, but in its essential motives, means, and aims the art of the earliest times is at one with the art of all times.[43]

Acknowledging the existence of consistency provided Grosse with a reasonable premise for seeking universally valid laws of art in the forms of primitive art. Perhaps driven by a similar recognition of uniformity, Warburg established a connection between the serpent ritual of American Indians and the classical motifs of European paganism. These enduring 'stereotype' were later transformed in Riegl's work into *Kunstwollen* that

[43] Ernst Grosse, *The Beginnings of Art*, p. 307.

travels through time and place. Following Grosse's logic, artworks persist qualitatively across generations, while their quantitative aspects evolve into various styles constrained by the era and region.

3. The Eye, the Body and the World

From Riegl's notes, we can observe that he often deliberately used the term *Kunstwollen* to replace the word 'style'; the conventional concept of style could not fully meet his needs.[44] This at least indicates that Riegl, like many art historians of his time, sought to address the problems of style in art with specific methodologies or theories.

In the nineteenth century, the discipline of art history borrowed various concepts and methods from other fields while striving to establish its own disciplinary autonomy. The study of style, which involves the visual sense, became an important category distinguishing art history from other disciplines. To shape its scientific nature, *Kunstwissenschaft* borrowed the concept of classification from natural sciences and applied it to the study of art history. For instance, in the preface to the sixth edition of *Principles of Art History*, Wölfflin stated that the purpose of basic concepts was not to provide value judgements but to establish a solid foundation for the characterization of style.[45] Beyond exploring the essence of artworks, *Kunstwissenschaft* also sought to uncover 'their internal organization and structure; it can accurately classify works according to their natural groups and establish genetic connections among works on the basis of their properties; it can arrive at an understanding of the historical events whose products it is studying and of the forces at work behind these events.'[46] If one aimed to find a reasonable taxonomy for the forms of artworks and reveal the laws of their evolution, then focusing on style would undoubtedly be the most effective and essential approach. Sedlmayr even declared that the aims of *Kunstwissenschaft* had been too much those of art history, and that its practice was almost equivalent to the history of style. However, Sedlmayr distinguished between internal and external style.[47]

[44] Alois Riegl, *Late Roman Art Industry*, p. XX.
[45] Heinrich Wölfflin, *Principles of Art History*, p. 78.
[46] Hans Sedlmayr, 'Toward a Rigorous Study of Art', p. 139.
[47] *Ibid.*, p. 154.

At the turn of the century, Riegl and his contemporaries Wickhoff and Wölfflin employed the methods of comparative analysis of artworks and formal analysis to grasp the principles of artistic development. Wölfflin was acquainted with several representatives of the Vienna School, and he maintained extensive correspondence with them. Joan Hart once discussed these three scholars in an article, positing therein that their research findings shared similar structures, namely, that they formed a stylistic dichotomy through polar opposites, from simple, circumscribed forms to complex, flamboyant ones.[48] Using opposing concepts to analyse artistic forms was, indeed, a trend in art history circles at the time, but Hart seemed to overlook the differences between Riegl and the others. Although Riegl proposed seemingly opposing formal concepts such as 'optic' and 'haptic', at a deeper level, he aligned more with the thinking of third-generation *Kunstwissenschaftlers*. This means he sought to understand such polar opposites on a epistemological level, rather than merely limiting himself to the comparative analysis of visual experiences. Of course, such formal opposition remained an important component of his observation methods.[49] Nevertheless, the influence of psychology on art history was a shared point among all three scholars. In the preface to the English version of *Die Spätrömische Kunstindustrie*, Rolf Winkes suggested that *Kunstwollen* was influenced by two things: on the one hand, by the philosophy of Schelling (1775–1854), Herbart, and Kant, and Hegel's concepts of *Zeitgeist* and worldview; on the other hand, Winkes also pointed out that Sigmund Freud (1856–1939) and Riegl taught in Vienna during the same period, implying an origin in psychology for the concept of *Kunstwollen*.[50]

These art historians reflected on modes of visual perception in their studies of style, all influenced by or responding to Hildebrand's theory. They believed that different modes of perception created different styles, and they viewed

[48] Joan Hart, 'Some Reflections on Wölfflin and the Vienna School', in *Wien und die Entwicklung der kunsthistorischen Methode*, Vienna: Böhlau, 1984, pp. 53–4.

[49] See Chapter 2.

[50] Rolf Winkes, 'Foreword', p. XIX. See also Kurt W. Forster, 'Monument/Memory and the Mortality of Architecture', in K. Michael Hays (ed.), *Oppositions Reader: Selected Essays 1973-1984*, New York: Princeton Architectural Press, 1998, p. 22.

psychology as the foundation for historical research.[51] It was precisely on this point that the problems of style became closely linked with psychological research in the nineteenth century.[52] Frankly, psychology not only provided a practical path of exploration for art history, or *Kunstwissenschaft*, but, according to Wilhelm Dilthey, it also laid practically the entire foundation for *Geisteswissenschaft* (broadly speaking, the humanities). Some even argued that psychology, one of the most important scientific methods for interpreting human civilisation and supporting the humanities, focused on the study of conscious or internal experience, whereas natural sciences concentrated on external experience.[53]

Today, Max Dessoir (1867–1947) is frequently regarded as a prominent figure in the field of Kunstwissenschaft. Yet, as the founder of the journal *Zeitschrift fur Ästhetik und allgemeine Kunstwissenschaft*, he was also a psychologist. In one of his books, he traced the history of psychology from ancient concepts of soul up to his own time. This, perhaps, provides a direct example for understanding the connection between *Kunstwissenschaft* and psychology.

However, for this discussion, Kant seems to be a more appropriate starting point, as the aesthetic tradition extending from his work has direct and close connections with the psychological approach in later art history.[54] Kant's *Kritik der reinen Vernunft* (1781) describes the relationship between rationalism and empiricism in philosophy by discussing the receptive and cognitive capacities of the mind. In terms of psychology, his philosophical model introduces two significant concepts: subjectivism and psychological nativism. Subjectivism derives from the concept of faculty dealing with

[51] Joan Hart, 'Some Reflections on Wölfflin and the Vienna School', pp. 53–4.

[52] It should be noted that in the nineteenth century, many scholars had different understandings of the term 'psychology', and sometimes different terms were used to discuss the scope of psychological research. Therefore, when I use the term 'psychology' in this book, I am not referring to a specific discipline but, rather, to various approaches to exploring the human mental world (including perceptual psychology), which may have used either the same or different terminology.

[53] Wilhelm Dilthey, 'Preface', in Rudolf A. Makkreel and Frithjof Rodi (eds), *Introduction to the Human Sciences*, trans. Michael Neville, Vol. 1, Princeton: Princeton University Press, 1989, pp. 47–52; Theodor Waitz, *Anthropologie der Naturvölker*, S. 6ff.

[54] Max Dessoir, *Geschichte der neueren deutschen Psychologie*, Berlin: Verlag von Carl Dunker, 1902 (Dessoir dedicated this book to Dilthey); See also the English translation by Donald Fisher, *Outlines of the History of Psychology*, New York: The Macmillan Company, 1912.

psychological phenomena, referring to the mind's representation of a reality independent of empirical reality; psychological nativism asserts that intuitions of time and space are a priori in the mind rather than acquired through experience. In his *Anthropologie in pragmatischer Hinsicht* (1798), Kant further elaborated on the faculties related to mind intuition and extended this faculty psychology into a form of cognitive psychology.[55] Many subsequent philosophers and psychologists recognised and emphasised the primary role of cognitive faculties in the process of perceiving forms.

Art historians did not literarily repeat Kant's ideas; rather, his theories were developed in a more materialistic direction, leading art historians to focus on how human physiological functions operated during the process of artistic creation and appreciation – a field of study that emerged from physiological psychology in the first half of the nineteenth century. Notable scholars in this field, particularly Helmholtz, Fechner, and Wundt, guided, to some extent the materialistic interpretation of Kant's a priori concepts. The transcendental elements in our sensory experience were no longer considered universal, continuous and pure forms in time and space; rather, they varied among individuals. This concept was similar to Kant's transcendental aesthetics, but it aligned with human organs. Differences in physiological structures led to variations in the transcendental structures of sensory experience. According to Andrea Pinotti,the reorganisation and adaptation of Kant's transcendental theories by *Kunstwissenschaft* manifested primarily in two aspects. First, since visual history focused on images, *Kunstwissenschaft* tended to regard the historical nature of the human body as being recorded in artworks; whether paintings, sculptures, architecture or crafts, all were products imbued with human sensory experience, thus reflecting historical information about human mental activity. The documentary meaning in Panofsky's iconology, proposed years later, can be seen as an extension of this line of though. In a similar sense, Warburg's concept of *Pathosformel* was considered a trace of human gestures and movements preserved in images. Secondly, since visual arts were inherently spatial arts, art history reflected the history of space,

[55] Katherine Arens, *Structures of Knowing: Psychologies of the Nineteenth Century*, Dordrecht, Boston, London: Kluwer Academic Publishers, 1989, p. 17.

that is, the spatial experiences of different groups across different periods. Following this thread, we see the development of various visual categories established by Wickhoff, Riegl, Wölfflin and others.[56]

Another philosopher who deserves to be mentioned is Arthur Schopenhauer (1788–1860), whose influence on the theoretical foundations of *Kulturwissenschaft* and *Kunstwissenschaft*, while perhaps not direct, at least worked subtly. His *Die Welt als Wille und Vorstellung* (1819) shaped nineteenth-century aesthetics in two ways: first, by endowing the aesthetic act of viewing with mental vitality; and, secondly, by emphasising the physiological nature of perception. The physiology of perception was also a new approach to aesthetics. Schopenhauer employed extensive physiological observations to support his metaphysical system. Creating an idea or image became a matter of neurological processes.[57] Schopenhauer remarked, 'What is *representation*? A very complicated *physiological* phenomenon in an animal's brain, whose result is the consciousness of a *picture* or *image* at that very spot.'[58] Meanwhile, by introducing spiritual subjectivity to the act of perception, Schopenhauer also established an animistic premise for discussing the *Kunstwollen* or other natural and cultural phenomena.

Kant's successor to the chair in Königsberg was Herbart, whose influence on the humanities, including art history, was far more significant then than it is now. In *Die Anfänge der Kunst*, Grosse tells us that the art philosophy of Hegel and Herbartianism were already outdated, but this observation indirectly highlights the authoritative position Herbart held in art studies.[59] Herbart's improvement was to reduce Kantian faculties and forms of perception, simplifying human consciousness into a continuous combination of forms and ideas. He also transformed complex aesthetic analysis into a formal theory. His psychological aesthetics combined Schopenhauer's 'objectivity' with Conrad Fiedler's (1841–1895) *Sichtbarkeit* ('visibility'), pursuing an

[56] Andrea Pinotti, 'Body-Building: August Schmarsow's *Kunstwissenschaft* Between Psychophysiology and Phenomenology', in Mitchell B. Frank and Daniel Adler (eds), *German Art History and Scientific Thought: Beyond Formalism*, Surrey: Ashgate, 2012, pp. 14–5.

[57] Harry Francis Mallgrave and Eleftherios Ikonomou, 'Introduction', in *Empathy, Form and Space*, pp. 9–10.

[58] Arthur Schopenhauer, *The World as Will and Representation*, Vol. 2, trans. E. F. J. Payne, New York: Dover Publications, Inc., 1969, p. 191.

[59] Ernst Grosse, *The Beginnings of Art*, p. 3.

absolutely objective and detached aesthetic framework that focused solely on problems of pure form. Herbart observed the ideas in human mind with an almost mathematical rationality similar to that of physiologists quantifying neurological behaviour. For instance, he meticulously analysed how people perceived space in visual arts through two phases – immediate and successive – though these rarely remained distinctly separate. At first glance, one perceived an overall phenomenon formed by various relationships of forms, then combined different concepts with the image, deriving three-dimensional space through a series of interrelated elements, such as the composition of blocks, intersections or parallel lines. Herbart believed relationships of forms were not simply external manifestations but that they also must engage with the viewer's imagination. Likewise, formal relationships were not simply external phenomena; they also had to engage the viewer's imagination. Therefore, he argued, we should include perception issues involving artistic judgment when discussing artworks.

Herbart's influence on intellectual society peaked in the mid-nineteenth century, following his death in 1841. His formal theory inspired the psychologist Adolf Zeising (1810–1876) to derive the formal significance of the golden ratio. Even music critic Eduard Hanslick (1825–1904) adopted some aspects of Herbart's psychological theory and popularised them through his writings.[60] Hanslick argued that the subject of music lay in its structure or form and that its essence was sound and movement. He regarded music as a formal language composed of elements such as harmonic progressions, variations, fluctuations and pauses, emphasising its intrinsic value. In *Die Lehre von den Tonempfindungen als physiologische Grundlage für die Theorie der Musik* (1863), Helmholtz praised Herbart and Hanslick for their attention to the essential elements of melody, noting that music aesthetics lacked scientific foundations for basic rules such as scales, chords, pitch and modes. Since music addressed human intuitive perception, Helmholtz naturally incorporated these questions into physiology. Fechner

[60] Julius von Schlosse, 'The Vienna School of the History of Art', p. 4; Eduard Hanslick, *Vom Musikalisch-Schönen*, Leipzig: Rudolph Weigel, 1854; English version *The Beautiful in Music: A Contribution to the Revisal of Musical Aesthetics*, trans. Gustav Cohen, London: Novello, 1891.

further developed Herbart's psychology, more rigorously quantifying the mathematical relationship between mind and body. In *Vorschule der Aesthetik* (1876), Fechner called for establishing a new aesthetics based on empirical evidence. His aesthetic approach resonated with his student Hermann Lotze (1817–1881), who wrote extensively on philosophy and physiology but shifted his focus gradually towards the conditions of human psychology.Finally, the explorations of Herbart, Helmholtz, Fechner and Lotze culminated in the work of Wundt, whose psychology laboratory marked the beginning of modern psychology. Wundt, who had once served as Helmholtz's assistant, transitioned from physiology to psychology. In *Grundzüge der physiologischen Psychologie* (1874) (Figure 18), he proclaimed psychology as a new scientific field initiated by Kant and Herbart. Like a surgeon, he directly explained visual reception through the physiological structure of the human body. He argued that the perception of colour involved muscle sensations, reflexes, binocular vision and neural activity. His distinctions among *Empfindung* ('sensation'), *Gefühl* ('feeling') and *Gemütsbewegung* ('emotional movement') shaped the theoretical framework for these concepts in the late nineteenth century. In addition, his concept of *Gedächtnisbild* ('memory image') formed the foundation for Adolf Göller's (1846–1902) development of stylistic forms.Wundt ultimately developed Herbart's ideal by establishing a quantifiable psychology. The remaining task was to develop Herbart's aesthetics into a comprehensive, rigorous science and system centred entirely on formal problems – a task undertaken by Robert Zimmermann.[61]

By then, through the efforts of Helmholtz, Fechner, Lotze, Wundt and others, a data- and experiment-based psychology had taken shape. Most of these scholars had medical backgrounds. The scientific approach they brought to psychology was precisely what the *Kunstwissenschaftlers* had been pursuing in the nineteenth century. The achievements of physiological psychology in visual perception studies attracted a group of *Kunstwissenschaftlers* who attempted to unlock the secrets of artistic rules.

[61] Harry Francis Mallgrave and Eleftherios Ikonomou, 'Introduction', pp. 11–5.

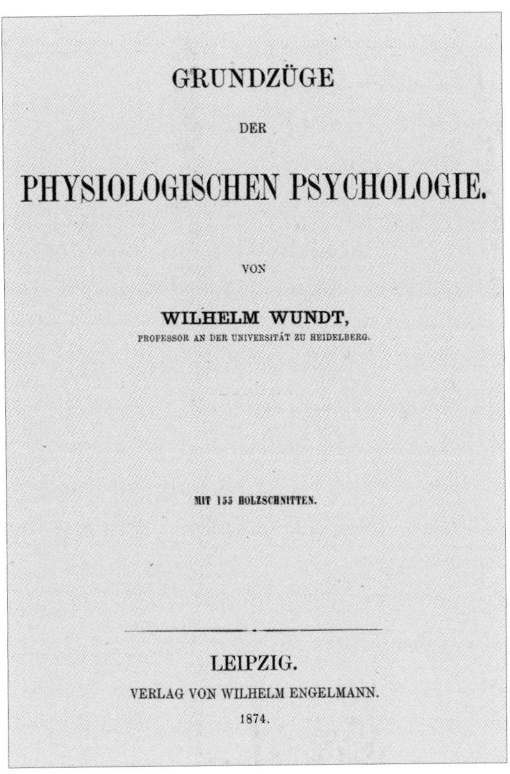

GRUNDZÜGE

DER

PHYSIOLOGISCHEN PSYCHOLOGIE.

VON

WILHELM WUNDT,

PROFESSOR AN DER UNIVERSITÄT ZU HEIDELBERG.

MIT 155 HOLZSCHNITTEN.

LEIPZIG.

VERLAG VON WILHELM ENGELMANN.

1874.

Figure 18. *Grundzüge der physiologischen Psychologie* by Wundt (1874)

Wundt had studied the concept of *Ausdrucksbewegung* ('expressive movement'), which almost instinctively brings to mind Warburg's *historische Psychologie des menschlichen Ausdrucks* ('historical psychology of human expression'). They both connect internal psychological emotions with the external expressions of the body. However, we must remember the influence of Friedrich Theodor Vischer (1807–1887) on Warburg in psychology and aesthetics. Wind noted that Warburg's theory of symbolic polarity was, in essence, a historical application of Friedrich Theodor Vischer's 1887 essay 'Das Symbol'.[62] In nineteenth-century psychology, the concept of the

[62] Edgar Wind, 'Warburg's Concept of *Kulturwissenschaft* and its Meaning for Aesthetics', p. 27.

symbol often appeared ambiguously as *Einfühlung* ('empathy'). The term *Einfühlung* has a significant tradition in the German intellectual world, where we find the subjective animism that contributed to Schopenhauer's idealism, along with the sensual perspective that incorporated Romantic description, as in the works of Novalis (1772–1801) and Friedrich Schlegel (1772–1829). Herder, also an early supporter of *Einfühlung* theory, responded to Kant's aesthetic theories. He emphasised in particular the symbolic and expressive value people attributed to natural forms – how to interpret all sensory *Erscheinung* through feeling and emotion. This subjective, animistic approach dominated some discussions of the phenomenal world in the mid-nineteenth century.[63]

In art history, Riegl viewed artistic development as an evolutionary process imbued with the vitality of animism. In his early academic career, Wölfflin showed similar tendencies. While we are familiar with his renowned formal analysis based on visual perception classification, in his earlier years, he was drawn more to the psychological aesthetics of the time. This interest inspired his doctoral dissertation *Prolegomena zu einer Psychologie der Architektur* (1886) (Figure 19). The tradition of anthropomorphising architecture can be traced back to at least Vitruvius, who attributed human characteristics to different architectural orders. This ancient tradition took a new psychological dimension in Wölfflin's account of architecture, perhaps informed by his reading of Semper's work.[64] In the conclusion of his dissertation, Wölfflin demonstrated his interest in formal psychology, revealing his later art historical research, progressing from the anthropomorphic representation of individual forms to the external expression of an entire collective. He began the chapter of his dissertation titled 'Principles of Historical Judgment' by stating: 'any architectural style reflects the attitude and movement of people in the period concerned. How people like to move and carry themselves is expressed above all in their costume, and it is not difficult to show that

[63] Harry Francis Mallgrave and Eleftherios Ikonomou, 'Introduction', p. 17–18.
[64] *Ibid*, p. 45.

architecture corresponds to the costume of its period.'[65] Wölfflin declared that only the rigorous and scientific methodology of psychology could provide a solid foundation for general historical studies. Thus, the delicate, rigid figures in Gothic painting and sculpture did not reflect the forms of architecture but rather the emotions underlying the artistic and architectural expressions. In *Renaissance und Barock* (1888), published two years later, Wölfflin extensively applied psychological interpretation, arguing that every era possessed a *Lebensgefühl* ('life-feeling') and that every style was imbued with emotion.[66] Similarly, Semper, in describing *Wellen* ornamentation, referred to it as a 'struggle between vitality and gravity',[67] while the Doric order was 'a structural symbol of monumental dignity'.[68] From the water vessels of the Greeks and Egyptians, Semper discerned cultural expressions and the bodily gestures of different peoples.[69] In this regard, Warburg's interpretations of *Pathosformel* and the embedded cultural memory from human gestures in both ancient and modern images undoubtedly resonated with the psychological approaches of his contemporaries in art history.

Warburg's expressive *formulas*, with symbolic value derived from image motifs, flourished in art history research under the influence of Friedrich Theodor Vischer's theories. However, Friederich had acknowledged that his *Das Symbol* owed much to his son, Robert. In the preface to his doctoral dissertation, Warburg had praised Robert Vischer highly, even placing his works before those of his father. Indeed, not only had Robert Vischer influenced Warburg, but his physiological psychology based on viewing

[65] Heinrich Wölfflin, 'Prolegomena zu einer Psychologie der Architektur', München: Kgl. Hof- & Universitäts-Buchdruckerei von Dr. C. Wolf & Sohn, 1886, S. 46; English version: 'Prolegomena to a Psychology of Architecture', in *Empathy, Form and Space*, p. 182.

[66] Heinrich Wölfflin, *Renaissance und Barock*, pp. 72–3. The Chinese translator translated *Lebensgefühl* as 生命意识, while the English translator, Kathrin Simon, indicated that the best English equivalent would be 'attitude to life'. To maintain consistency with Wundt's earlier adoption of the term *Gefühl*, I translate it as 感受 ('feeling/sensation').

[67] Gottfried Semper, 'On the Origin of Some Architectural Styles', *RES: Anthropology and Aesthetics*, Vol. 9 (Spring 1985), pp. 53–67.

[68] Gottfried Semper, *Style in the Technical and Tectonic Arts; or, Practical Aesthetics*, Los Angeles: the Getty Research Institute, 2004, p. 800; Gottfried Semper, *Der Stil in den technischen und tektonischen Künsten oder praktische Ästhetik*, Bd. 2, München: Friedrich Bruckmann's Verlag, 1863, S. 464.

[69] Gottfried Semper, *Style in the Technical and Tectonic Arts; or, Practical Aesthetics*, pp. 468–9.

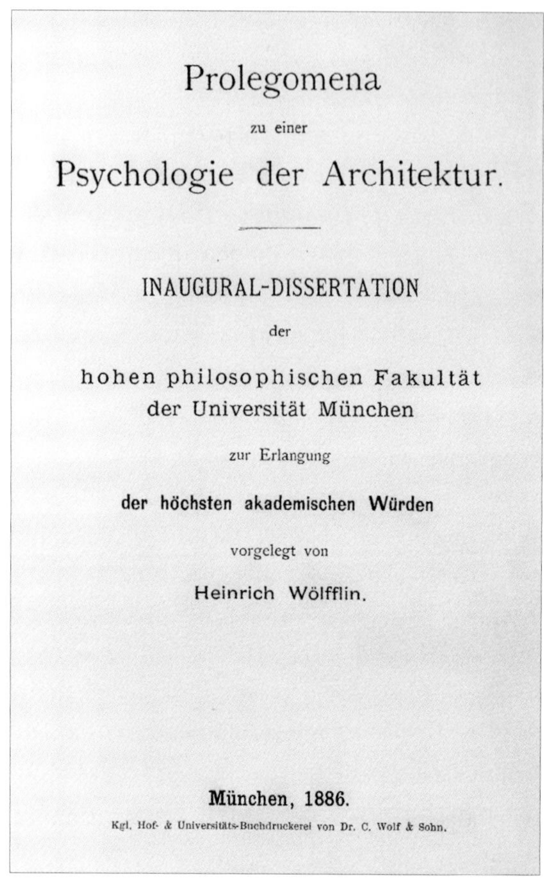

Prolegomena

zu einer

Psychologie der Architektur.

INAUGURAL-DISSERTATION

der

hohen philosophischen Fakultät
der Universität München

zur Erlangung

der höchsten akademischen Würden

vorgelegt von

Heinrich Wölfflin.

München, 1886.

Kgl. Hof- & Universitäts-Buchdruckerei von Dr. C. Wolf & Sohn.

Figure 19. *Prolegomena zu einer Psychologie der Architektur* by Wölfflin (1886)

mechanisms could also be said to have paved new paths for *Kunstwissenschaft*.

As the organ most directly involved in visual perception, the eye was a primary focus for physiological psychologists and *Kunstwissenschaftlers*, inspiring some of the earliest collaborations between art history and psychology. Helmholtz regarded movement as a fundamental factor in perception, not merely recording experience but actively constructing it. Both sighted and blind people could develop spatial intuition regardless of vision, because hand movement and touch helped the body to capture spatial sense.[70] Vision itself is inherently dynamic, not only because we can direct our gaze here or there but also because seeing near and far involves movement. This is determined by the adjustment mechanism of the lens, which changes its curvature to focus: when looking at something close, the front surface of the lens becomes more curved; when looking into the distance, it flattens.[71] Following his investigation into the viewing mechanisms of the eye, Robert Vischer postulated the closest connection between physiology and art studies. Inspired by Wundt's *Vorlesungen über die Menschen- und Thierseele* (1863), Vischer wrote his famous work *Über das optische Formgefühl* (1873) (Figure 20). In the preface, Vischer cited his father's statement that the mystery he faced 'has to be explained by physiology in conjunction with psychology'.[72] As Hermann Glöckner (1889–1987) noted, *Über das optische Formgefühl* can be considered a study in physiological psychology.[73] Indeed, Robert Vischer was interested in art history, later advocating in *Kunstgeschichte und Humanismus* (1880) for breaking down barriers between art history and aesthetics through the use of philosophically classified empiricism. *Über das optische Formgefühl* was crucial in bridging between physiological psychology and art history research. This book can be regarded as the theoretical point of departure for *Kunstwissenschaftlers* such as Riegl, Wölfflin and Schmarsow, whose explorations of form were, in some sense, all based on the categorisation of visual perception applied to works of art.

Robert Vischer emphasised the physiological mechanisms of the body involved in conditioned sensory and emotional responses. The foundation of his theory of *Einfühlung* lies in the distinction between *Empfindung* and *Gefühl*. The former is merely the body's physical response to external stimuli;

[70] Hermann von Helmholtz, *Die Thatsachen in der Wahrnehmung: Rede gehalten zur Stiftungfeier der Friedrich-Wilhelms-Universität zu Berlin am 3. August 1878*, Berlin: A. Hirschwald, 1879; English version, Russell Kahl (ed.), *Selected Writings of Hermann von Helmholtz*, Connecticut: Wesleyan University Press, 1971.

[71] J. P. C. Southall, *Helmholtz's Treatise on Physiological Optics*, New York: Dover Publications, 1962.

[72] Robert Vischer, Über *das optische Formgefühl: ein Beitrag zur Aesthetik*, Leipzig: Hermann Credner, 1873, S. VIII; English version: 'On the Optical Sense of Form: A Contribution to Aesthetics', in *Empathy, Form and Space*, p. 92. Friedrich Theodor Vischer, 'Kritik meiner Ästhetik', in *Kritische Gänge*, Vol. 5, Stuttgart: Cotta, 1866, S. 142.

[73] Hermann Glockner, 'Robert Vischer und die Krisis der Geisteswissenschaften im letzten Drittel des neunzehnten Jahrhunderts', *Logos: Internationale Zeitschrift für Philosophie der Kultur*, 15 (1926), S. 47–102.

the latter involves activities of the mind or emotions. Sensations can be further divided into *Zuempfindung* ('direct sensation') and *Nachempfindung* ('reactive sensation'). *Zuempfindung* is the immediate sensory response to external stimuli, while Nachempfindung involves the activity of nerves and muscles. When discussing the act of viewing, Robert Vischer aligned these two sensory processes with two types of viewing: *Sehen* ('seeing') and *Schauen* ('scanning'). *Sehen* is a relatively unconscious response to visual stimuli that causes neural vibrations – passive images received by the visual organs; it is the visual sensation at the first glimpse, similar to a vague overall impression. This type of viewing requires no special effort; it is merely a physiological activity produced by neural tension, where the mind first senses the flash of an internal concept. This preliminary step is decisive for all artistic intuition; in other words, it is the 'eye' that an artist must possess.

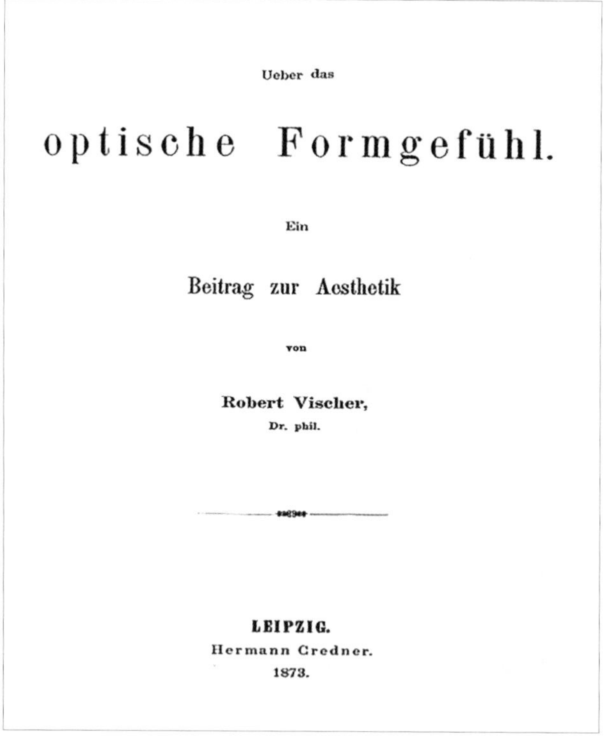
Ueber das

optische Formgefühl.

Ein

Beitrag zur Aesthetik

von

Robert Vischer,
Dr. phil.

LEIPZIG.
Hermann Credner.
1873.

Figure 20. *Über das optische Formgefühl* (1873) by Robert Vischer

Schauen, on the other hand, is a more focused way of viewing, where the eye actively engages, no longer relying on natural impulses, to grasp a relatively complete whole. Viewing the observed object from top to bottom and left to right, the eye explores the boundaries of forms to establish relationships between individual dimensions. In this process, Robert Vischer identified two methods of *Schauen*. The first is linear, involving the fingertips defining the contours of an object. The second involves the overall mapping of multiple surfaces, as if the hand traces over various planes, over convexity and concavity, the path of light, mountain slopes, ridges and hollows. *Schauen* is more conscious than *Sehen*; it demands a dialectical analysis of form, involving the breaking down or connecting of elements to organise their dynamic relationships. Into the process of *Schauen* Robert Vischer incorporated more conscious and subjective factors from the observer. From an animistic perspective, he acknowledged that *Schauen* might contribute to a complete artistic presentation. He described this eye movement as bringing life to dead phenomena – a rhythmic revival. He placed *Schauen* above *Sehen*, viewing it as a higher-level repetition of the impressions formed during *Sehen*.[74] Moreover, Robert Vischer's theory included a more advanced viewing which required mental representation and imagination, through which he established connections with *Einfühlung*.

If Robert Vischer's classification of viewing behaviour based on physiological psychology inspired new perspectives for the study of visual arts, then Hildebrand directly provided a theory source for the methodology of art history at the turn of the century. Twenty years after the publication of *Über das optische Formgefühl*, Hildebrand released *Das Problem der Form in der bildenden Kunst* (1893) (Figure 21).[75] However, we must briefly mention Fiedler, as it was his acquaintance with the sculptor Hildebrand in the 1860s that led him to abandon his legal career and turn to studying the philosophy and art. These two figures are often discussed together, not

[74] Robert Vischer, Über das optische Formgefühl, S. 2–3; English version 'On the Optical Sense of Form: A Contribution to Aesthetics', pp. 93–4.

[75] Adolf von Hildebrand, *Das Problem der Form in der bildenden Kunst*, Strassburg: Heitz, 1893; English version, *The Problem of Form in Painting and Sculpture* (New York: G. E. Stechert & Co., 1907), trans. Max Meyer and Robert Morris Ogden.

only because of their deep friendship but also due to their close intellectual exchange. Hildebrand's book owed much to Fiedler's theory and his views on art. Their correspondence reveals that Hildebrand began sending drafts of *Das Problem der Form in der bildenden Kunst* to Fiedler for review as early as 1881. Fiedler would often respond with detailed commentaries, addressing both the content and the logical structure, prompting Hildebrand to revise his manuscript several times.[76]

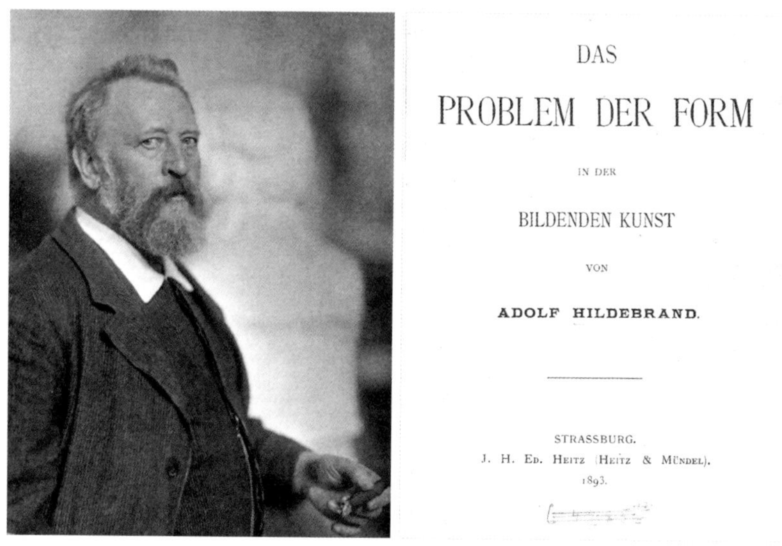

Figure 21. Hildebrand and his *Das Problem der Form in der bildenden Kunst* (1893)

Fiedler's theory of art was philosophically based on the aesthetics of Kant, Schopenhauer and Herbart. He seemed to reject observing art through any external means or perspectives, arguing instead that studying art through predetermined rules would only lead to a superficial understanding of form. Analysing art from cultural and historical perspectives, he believed, could never allow one to grasp the creative essence of art. For Fiedler, the problem of

[76] For information about Hildebrand's writing and manuscript revisions, see Henning Bock's 'Introduction' in *Adolf von Hildebrand: Gesammelte Schriften zur Kunst*, Cologne: Westdeutscher Verlag, 1969, pp. 17–33.

form could be resolved only through art itself; in other words, the core of his theory lay in *Sichtbarkeit* ('visibility'). *Das Problem der Form in der bildenden Kunst* explores the relationship between form and external appearance and their influence on artistic representation. In the preface, Hildebrand stated explicitly that concepts of art or representations of form differed from our shared understanding of form and space, and the relationship between form and appearance was reflected in this distinction. The essence of the issue also concerns *Sichtbarkeit*, as the act of creating art is one thing, and the process of creation quite another. People's focus on creating often leads them to pay excessive attention to technical procedures, thus neglecting how an object is brought into being and failing to recognise that image-making is an intellectual activity. When artists represent the world through form, they should not concentrate solely on external appearance; instead, they should understand how appearance expresses its content of form through perceptual processes.[77] In addition to Fiedler, Hildebrand also referred to the works of physiological and psychological scholars such as Wundt and Helmholtz; in particular, his distinction between distant and near view closely resembled Robert Vischer's *Sehen* and *Schauen*.

The first chapter of *Das Problem der Form in der bildenden Kunst* is 'Geschichtsvorstellung und Bewegungsvorstellung'. In this chapter, Hildebrand distinguishes between visual perception and kinesthetic perception, thereby clarifying the conceptual differences between the the visual and the kinesthetic. The earliest English translator used the term 'kinesthetic' for *Bewegung*, explaining in a note that 'By kinesthetic we mean pertaining to sensations of movement, in this case, eye movement.'[78] Visual perception referred to distant viewing with a static eye, while kinesthetic perception was related to near viewing, where the eyes must engage in a series of movements to grasp the entire object. This is because distant objects are always two-dimensional on the retina, whereas our experience of three-dimensional or sculptural form sometimes requires a temporal process for complete perception – either through physiological or kinesthetic movement.

[77] Adolf von Hildebrand, 'The Problem of Form in the Fine Arts', in *Empathy, Form and Space*, pp. 227–8.

[78] Adolf von Hildebrand, *The Problem of Form in Painting and Sculpture*, p. 21.

When viewing a distant object, its overall surface can be viewed at a glance. Up close, the observer sees only a particular section, gradually shifting the position of the eyes to integrate other surfaces into a whole. As Hildebrand stated:

> If his vantage point is distant, the eyes no longer converge at an angle but view the object in parallel lines. Then the overall image is two-dimensional, for the third dimension (all closer and more distant parts within the object's appearance) or the modeled object can be perceived only by surface contrasts: that is, as surface features indicating distance or nearness. If the observer steps closer to the object, he will need a different visual accommodation to see the given object; he will cease taking in the overall appearance at one glance and can compose the image only by moving the eyes back and forth and making various accommodations. He will therefore divide the overall appearance into several visual impressions that are connected by the movements of his eyes. The closer the observer comes to the object, the more eye movements he will need, and the less coherent will be the visual impression. Finally the field of vision becomes so confined that he will be able to focus only on one point at a time, and he will experience the spatial relationships between different points by moving his eyes. Now seeing becomes scanning, the resulting ideas are not visual [*Gesichtsvorstellungen*] but kinesthetic [*Bewegungsvorstellungen*]; they supply the material for an abstract vision and idea of form.[79]

In other words, in near viewing, *Schauen* transforms into a genuine touching and kinesthetic action. For Robert Vischer, *Sehen* corresponded to distant viewing, representing the first overall impression of an object; *Schauen* corresponded to near viewing, requiring active exploration by the eyes across various surfaces of the object. Here, we cannot help but associate these two viewing modes with the classification category in *Kunstwissenschaft*. In near viewing or *Schauen*, the eyes function much like the fingertips, touching the details of the image; isn't this the theoretical origin of the optic and

[79] Adolf von Hildebrand, 'The Problem of Form in the Fine Arts', p. 229.

tactile in art and image theory at that time? Riegl and Wölfflin adopted and further developed the viewing antitheses of Vischer and Hildebrand for art history research. In Riegl's framework, near viewing manifested as the tactile representation of Egyptian art, while distant viewing characterised the overall features of Roman visual art. Wölfflin associated near viewing with the linear style of Renaissance art; distant viewing connected to the painterly style of Baroque art. However, it is noteworthy that antitheses of forms like Riegl's 'haptic' and 'optic' or Wölfflin's 'linear' and 'painterly' overemphasise the visual factors in perception, thereby simplifying it into a dialectical game dominated solely by the eyes.

Before introducing his famous five pairs of concepts in an incomplete form,[80] Wölfflin praised Hildebrand in *Die Klassische Kunst* (1899), stating that Hildebrand brought a new method for studying art that aided the discovery of *künstlerischer Inhalt* ('artistic content') or *innere Gesetze* ('inner laws').[81] Although he believed in the connection between the architecture of the Italian Renaissance and the humanist ideals, we should first study the visual category to fully understand the artistic phenomena of that time. As mentioned earlier, while preparing his doctoral dissertation, Wölfflin had initially acknowledged the importance of psychology and observed the forms of artworks with animistic overtones of empathy, yet he was barely affected by Hildebrand's theories at that time. It was only around the decade before the publication of *Die Klassische Kunst*, after becoming acquainted with Fiedler and Hildebrand, that he began to appreciate their theories. That year, in a letter to his parents, Wölfflin conveyed his joy, as Hildebrand had expressed his admiration for the writing style and the content of his work.[82]

As a student of Zimmermann, Riegl transformed the Herbartian distinction between 'optical' and 'tactile' into a polar opposites in art

[80] On 7 December 1911, Wölfflin delivered the lecture 'Das Problem des Stils in der bildenden Kunst' at the Royal Prussian Academy of Sciences. The manuscript was published in the 1912 *Sitzungsberichte der königlich preußischen Akademie der Wissenschaften*. In this lecture, Wölfflin introduced ideas of his five pairs of concepts.

[81] Heinrich Wölfflin, *Die Klassische Kunst: Eine Einführung in die italienische Renaissance*, München: F. Bruckmann A.-G.: 1924, S. VIII.

[82] Joseph Gantner (Hrg.), *Heinrich Wölfflin, 1864-1945: Autobiographie, Tagebücher und Briefe*, Basel: Benno Schwabe, 1982, pp. 67–8.

historical research.[83] In other words, Riegl was influenced by Herbart through his teacher, Zimmermann. As previously mentioned, Herbart, from a physiological perpective, had discovered two stages in visual perception that approximate what would later be described as distant and near viewing. Although he had not adopted the terminology of Vischer or Hildebrand, he had expressed similar ideas through immediate and successive perception, namely, first seeing the whole formed by relationships of forms, then noticing a series of interconnected elements to comprehend three-dimensional space. Zimmermann systematised the formal aesthetics he had inherited from Herbart, and he applied Helmholtz's experiments on the mathematical relationships in musical harmony to visual arts.

From Herbart onwards, we see an aesthetic development following the visibility of images, as many psychologists and physiologists either moved away from or transformed the metaphysical aesthetic speculation of pure contemplation from Kant. This attention to the process of image perception and the classification of visual forms had entered the methodological framework of art history by the second generation of *Kunstwissenschaftlers*. It had finally completed its transformation to phenomenology by the third generation of *Kunstwissenschaftlers*, in the twentieth century. This shift also reflected the development of aesthetics itself.[84]

Following Herbart, Riegl brought formal aesthetics into his discussions on style. As Schlosser remarked, 'our Vienna had been the final fortress of Herbartianism into the final third of the 19th Century.'[85] In his classic work on the history of art writing, Venturi devoted an entire chapter to the concept of visualisation, tracing from Herbart to Riegl and Wölfflin. Although Venturi could not confirm whether there was a direct theoretical interaction between Riegl and Fiedler, he indicated that they both acknowledged the formalism of Herbartianism. He also identified a connection between Riegl and

[83] William M. Johnston, *The Austrian Mind: An Intellectual and Social History 1848-1938*, Berkeley, Los Angeles, London: University of California Press, 1972, p. 289.
[84] Lambert Wiesing, *The Visibility of the Image: History and Perspectives of Formal Aesthetics*, trans. Nancy Ann Roth, New York: Bloomsbury Academic, 2016, p. 9. For the original German version, see *Die Sichtbarkeit des Bildes: Geschichte und Perspektiven der formalen Ästhetik*, Rowohlt Taschenbuch Verlag, 1997.
[85] Julius von Schlosser, 'The Vienna School of the History of Art', p. 4.

Herbart in the concept of *Kunstwollen*, stating that Riegl firmly believed in the possibility of establishing various a priori types within the Herbartianism tradition as principles of stylistic change under *Kunstwollen*. This tradition, according to Venturi, was concerned with discussing the tactile and optical characteristics of objects themselves, and their presence in space, in objective and subjective perception.[86]

Beyond Riegl and Wölfflin, another representative of *Kunstwissenschaft*, Schmarsow, relied heavily on the achievements of physiological psychology. Despite sharing common theoretical sources, Riegl and Wölfflin inherited their focus on vision from Robert Vischer and Hildebrand, while Schmarsow emphasised movement, considering vision to be a changing or dynamic behaviour. Vischer and Hildebrand were influenced by Wundt and Helmholtz, respectively, both of whom emphasised the importance of movement; the body in physiological psychology was essentially conceived as the body in movement. Wundt developed the concept of *Ausdrucksbewegung*, linking expressions of the mind to the imitation of dynamic actions. The two extremes he identified were both related to movement: emotions under highly active neural states, and emotions under near-paralytic states. In contrast, Helmholtz straightforwardly declared that movement was the foundation of perception. Although Robert Vischer's and Hildebrand's primary legacy in art history lies in the classifications for visual perception modes, they also acknowledged the role of the body in the perceptual process. Hildebrand stated that our sympathy with the external world enabled us to understand any experience through bodily analogy. As he put it, 'we animate and denote every new appearance we encounter with the physical feelings that have accompanied similar appearances in the past.'[87] Robert Vischer also noted that visual stimuli not only required eye experience but it also involved other parts of the body, even demanding the engagement of the entire body.[88] In this sense, Wölfflin aligned more closely with this perspective of perceiving objects through the body ('Our own bodily organization is the form through

[86] Lionello Venturi, *History of Art Criticism*, p. 281.
[87] Adolf von Hildebrand, 'The Problem of Form in the Fine Arts', p. 261.
[88] Robert Vischer, 'On the Optical Sense of Form: A Contribution to Aesthetics', pp. 98–9.

which we apprehend everything *physical*').[89] However, in his later work, Wölfflin shifted his focus towards vision.

Schmarsow took a more decisive stance than Wölfflin, not only opposing the binary opposition in visual classification but also denying that humans were merely visual beings who observed the world from a fixed viewpoint. In the process of perceiving the world and observing objects, people are constantly changing their positions, altering their perspectives, or examining an object in their hands to grasp its overall shape. Although Hildebrand also used the term 'kinesthetic', he emphasised the movement of the eyes, whereas Schmarsow used 'kinesthetic' to refer to the movement of the entire body. Schmarsow regarded the body as an organised intermediary between the subject and the external environment. The structure of the body, its upright posture, the coordination between hands and arms and feet and legs, and its internal visual organs all work together to determine our sense of orientation, shape our modes of construction and production, and are connected to all our actions.[90]

Through perceiving the world via body movement, Schmarsow established corresponding relationships between the body and the formal values of visual artworks across different dimensions such as vertical, horizontal and depth.[91] In his study of architecture, Schmarsow expanded the traditional approach of discussing form through spatial perception by introducing the factor of body movement, thereby integrating time into space. Only when the human body moves in its interior can one perceive the depth of architecture. The interaction between time and space thus creates the concept of rhythm. Schmarsow referenced Lotze's physiological studies, which suggested that encountering an absolutely uniform sequence of equal intervals in time could cause discomfort, prompting individuals to spontaneously develop

[89] Heinrich Wölfflin, 'Prolegomena to a Psychology of Architecture', pp. 157–8.

[90] August Schmarsow, *Grundbegriffe der Kunstwissenschaft: am Übergang vom Altertum zum Mittelalter kritisch erörtert und in systematischem Zusammenhange dargestellt*, Leipzig: Teubner, 1905, S. 33.

[91] Schmarsow's 'scientific system' of modes of perception and formal values laid a foundation for the epistemological framework for *Kunstwissenschaft* later developed by figures such as Panofsky, Wind and the Vienna School of Art History. In contrast, Schmarsow's contemporaries in *Kunstwissenschaft*, such as Riegl or Wölfflin, were also attempting to study art through scientific methods. They had not yet taken as radical an approach as Schmarsow in constructing a self-contained conceptual system for art historical research.

their own sense of rhythm to counteract this unease. Even the varying pace and duration of breathing constituted a form of rhythm, which was crucial to the sense of time experienced by our organs. Similar ideas can be found in Hildebrand's writings. He also emphasised the significance of rhythm. Even Wölfflin, in his doctoral dissertation, explicitly linked the rhythm of breathing to different sensations of interior space.[92]

Thus, echoing the Hegelian and animism theory, Schmarsow asserted that each type of rhythm corresponded to a specific *Weltanschauung* ('worldview'). Inspired by psychology and physiology, it was common practice among *Kunstwissenschaftlers* of that period to link the artistic style of a specific era with the *Weltanschauung* of its time. Riegl, Wölfflin and Panofsky all followed this approach, though with different points of focus: Riegl focused on *Kunstwollen*, Wölfflin on the comparative study of paired formal categories, and Panofsky on the intrinsic meaning of the third level of iconology, while Schmarsow defined art as the product of humans' creative engagement with the world.[93] Furthermore, Schmarsow may also have been influenced by biology, as he explicitly referenced Jakob von Uexküll (1864–1944) and works such as *Umwelt und Innenwelt der Tiere* (1910) and *Bausteine zu einer biologischen Weltanschauung* (1913).[94] Uexküll believed that although different species lived in the same world, they possessed different senses of time and space because their varying body organisations lead to variations in perceptions of the world. In other words, the subject does not passively recognise a pre-existing world but, rather, actively constructs its unique world in this process.

Edmund Husserl (1859–1938) once used the term 'style' to describe our cognitive attitudes towards the world. Although he did not refer specifically to artistic meanings, he still used *Einstellung* ('attitude') – a habitually fixed

[92] Adolf von Hildebrand, 'The Problem of Form in the Fine Arts', pp. 247–8; Heinrich Wölfflin, 'Prolegomena to a Psychology of Architecture', p. 169.

[93] '...schöpferische Auseinandersetzung des Menschen mit der Welt', August Schmarsow, *Grundbegriffe der Kunstwissenschaft*, S.33. In fact, at the end of the nineteenth century, Riegl also expressed a similar view: 'Thus, all of humanity's creative artworks ultimately amounts to nothing more than a "Wettschaffe,"' Alois Riegl, *Historical Grammar of Visual Arts*, p. 2.

[94] August Schmarsow, 'Kunstwissenschaft und Kulturphilosophie mit gemeinsamen Grundbegriffen', *Zeitschrift für Ästhetik und allgemeine Kunstwissenschaft*, 13 (1919), S. 231–2.

style of the will– to express the relationship between humans and the world. His idea was straightforward:

> The human spirit, after all, is grounded on the human physis; each individual human psychic life is founded upon corporeality, and thus each community upon the bodies of the individual human beings who are members of it. So if a truly exact explanation of the phenomena of the humanistic disciplines is to be possible, and accordingly a far-reaching scientific praxis similar to that in the natural sphere, the humanists must not only consider the spirit as spirit but must also go back to the corporeal basis'.[95]

Husserl's concept of *Einstellung* includes the direction of the will or various interests determined by style, as well as ultimate ends, which, in turn, shape the overall style of cultural accomplishments. Individual life is also determined through its interaction with style, while the specific contents of culture changes in accordance with a relatively enclosed historical process. Humanity, or a particular nation or tribe, always lives under some attitude in its historical context, and their life consistently exhibits a normative style.[96] Many scholars have discussed the connection between Riegl's concept of *Kunstwollen* and Husserl's theories, and the possibility of such a connection can also be observed here. The artistic style of each era originates from its specific *Kunstwollen*, and the existence of different *Kunstwollen* stems from the varying manifestations of underlying basic *Einstellung* across different times and places. Husserl's theories later influenced the study of multiple spatial experiences in phenomenological psychiatry, meaning that some bodies transcended the specific *Einstellung* of their era and developed more than one spatiotemporal perception. Ludwig Binswanger (1881–1966) was an expert in studying the relationship

[95] Edmund Husserl, 'Philosophy and the Crisis of European Humanity', in *The Crisis of European Sciences and Transcendental Phenomenology, : An Introduction to Phenomenological Philosophy*, trans. David Carr, Evanston: Northwestern University Press, 1970. p. 271.

[96] Edmund Husserl, 'Philosophy and the Crisis of European Humanity', p. 280.

between these multiple spatiotemporal experiences and psychopathology; and Warburg was once a patient at his clinic.

When his contemporaries were immersed in the new findings of physiological psychology, whether focusing on the mechanisms of visual perception or the correspondence between the body and *Weltanschauung*, Warburg remained sceptical of this formalist art history that relied entirely on perceptual patterns. This could be viewed as a significant watershed between *Kulturwissenschaft* and *Kunstwissenschaft*, although they shared much of the same knowledge and theoretical foundations. However, as we have seen, *Kunstwissenschaftlers* of that time, motivated by an urgent need to establish the autonomy of their discipline, often simplified complex questions of art history into mere questions of visual form. For example, from Wölfflin's perspective, different cognitive modes of visual perception between individuals of the Renaissance and Baroque periods gave rise to their respective styles. In this view, the formal style was in parallel to the cultural context or historical background of its time. In his essay defending Warburg's methodological approach, Wind explicitly states that if we view different categories of culture as parallel, we overlook the forces generated through their interaction. Without these forces, the dynamic development of history becomes difficult to comprehend. Furthermore, Wind opposes the idea of 'pure vision', arguing that all acts of viewing are conditioned by their environment and could never be isolated from the experiential context. In Wind's view, Warburg had chosen the correct third path: instead of positing inner connections from abstract viewpoints, he studied individual objects where those connections could be grasped in history. This is why Warburg admired Jacob Burckhardt (1818–1897) and sought to uncover the factors within cultural milieus that determined the formation of style. Warburg believed that any attempt to separate the connections of image with religion, poetry, cult and drama would cut the lifeblood of image.[97]

Moreover, there is another, more subtle difference between Warburg and the *Kunstwissenschaftlers*. Although Warburg also focused on the movement of the body, he did not refer to the movement of the viewer or the artist

[97] Edgar Wind, 'Warburg's Concept of *Kulturwissenschaft* and its Meaning for Aesthetics', pp. 24–5.

during the process of perception. Instead, he focused on the movement of the figures within the images – what he referred to as the gestural movements of *Pathosformeln*. In this regard, Warburg's most direct theoretical sources were Charles Darwin and Theodor Piderit (1826–1912). In 1888, he wrote a note on Darwin's *The Expression of the Emotions in Man and Animals* (1872): 'At last a book which helps me.'[98] Forty years later, in a lecture, he said:

> To conceive of human expression in visual art as a template for a practical and active life – be it as a religious cult or as the drama of court ceremonial or indeed the theatre – is an idea I have wanted to develop for a long time. It first came to me through my encounter with two books that I read during my time in Florence in 1888, entirely independently of one another and without any hope of them ever directly feeding into my thoughts on art history. These books were Darwin's *On the Expression of Mind* and Piderit's *Mimik und Physiognomik*. The fact that the general facial expression is a reflexively repeated expression reacting to a purely intellectual stimulus … an example: if one dislikes somebody, one pull's one's mouth as if one were tasting something sour.[99]

Warburg expanded this theory of memory traces left by expressive stimuli and applied it to the observation of geographical and national contexts. He applied Darwin's theory of memory about traces of stimuli to explain the causes of stylistic changes. Thus, he identified what he saw as 'foreign influence' in Italian art akin to the imprints of external stimuli.[100]

However, we cannot assume that Warburg's insights into expressive movements came entirely from Darwin just because of Warburg's differences from his contemporary *Kunstwissenschaftlers*. As mentioned earlier, Warburg

[98] In fact, he transcribed this marginal note from his diary into the book: '*Endlich ein Buch, das mir hilft.*' E.H. Gombrich, *Aby Warburg*, p. 72. The copy of *The Expression of Emotions in Man and Animals* that was owned by Warburg is now preserved in the Warburg Institute in London.

[99] Aby Warburg, 'Vom Arsenal zum Laboratorium', S. 687. English version: Sabine Flach, 'Communicating Vessels: 'On the Development of a Theory of Representation in Darwin and Warburg', in Barbara Larson and Sabine Flach (eds), *Darwin and Theories of Aesthetics and Cultural History*, p. 109.

[100] Aby Warburg, 'Vom Arsenal zum Laboratorium', p. 687.

admired and absorbed the achievements of psychologists, as many of his fellow art historians did, but he also referenced the work of Robert Vischer in his notes. However, from the same foundations, he took a different path.[101] When Warburg read Darwin's work in Florence in 1888, he was attending a seminar led by Schmarsow on Masaccio (1401–1428) and Italian sculpture. It was through Schmarsow that Warburg was introduced to Wundt's theories. Under Wundt's influence, Schmarsow developed the view that studying facial expressions or gestures required first understanding the movements of expression. He established a genetic pedigree of artistic activities by a priori structure. According to this logic, words are a synthesis of gesture and sound, and gestures and sounds must have existed prior to language. Thus, images are abstractions from objects and space, both of which must predate the history of images. Therefore, mime and sculpture are the ancestors of all subsequent artistic activities, while architecture and music represent further developments in space and time. In practical contexts, 'any movement of the body is an unintentional expressive movement'.[102] For Schmarsow, Wundt's *Völkerpsychologie* (1900–1920) laid the most important foundation for *Kunstwissenschaft*. Through movements existing in nature, we find traces of primitive emotions in the gestures and expressions in the artistic world.[103] Thus, we can understand why Schmarsow defined art as 'Man's attempt, through his creation, to come to terms with the world in which he finds himself'. His essay *Kunstwissenschaft und Völkerpsychologie* undoubtedly became an important document for understanding Warburg's early thoughts on expressive movement.[104]

Schmarsow's statement also reveals traces of the characteristics of animism. The concept of animism has a long history; it exerted a profound influence on art researchers through the writings of Schopenhauer and was later discussed by the anthropologist Edward Tylor, most notably in his *Primitive Culture* (Fig. 22). Those who held this implicit attitude essentially presupposed that everything in nature possessed a spiritual essence. As a

[101] Aby Warburg, 'Sandro Botticellis, Geburt der Venus "und, Frühling"', in *Gesammelte Schriften*, S. 5.
[102] E.H. Gombrich, *Aby Warburg*, pp. 40-41.
[103] August Schmarsow, 'Kunstwissenschaft und Völkerpsychologie', S. 318–9.
[104] E.H. Gombrich, *Aby Warburg*, pp. 40–41.

result, as seen in Riegl's *Kunstwollen* and early Wölfflin's architecture, they studied objects as entities with their own lives. In a sense, it was this animistic premise that allowed scholars like Riegl to view minor artworks – whether ornament patterns or non-European artefacts – with the same seriousness with which they approached traditional fine art.[105] The consciousness of animism objectively undermined the validity of the traditional system of art evaluation and shifted the core issue of style onto the will of all peoples across all epochs.

Robert Vischer's theory of *Einfühlung* distinguished between passive physiological perception and active emotional projection. From the perspective of animism, we can see how he contributed to establishing the concept of artistic impulse. In his view, connecting with the world through *pantheïstische Drang* ('pantheistic desire') formed the foundation of emotion: 'This symbolizing activity can be based on nothing other than the pantheistic urge for union with the world, which can by no means be limited to our more easily understood kinship with the human species but must, consciously or unconsciously, be directed toward the universe.'[106] Robert Vischer believed that the empathetic impulse arose from humanity's psychological attempt to connect with nature. This impulse reflected humanity's inability to tolerate barriers and its desire to wander through the world freely, feeling integrated into and participating in its harmonious order. Even under the most primitive conditions, artists imitate not nature but, rather, the hidden universal life vitality – the manifestation of their own spiritual life or pure self. The sentiment was considered as a spiritual activity that assumes external form as symbols of its existence. Thus, art becomes the objectification of humanity in sensory and harmonious forms. For art historians, analysing artworks requires the intervention of emotional symbols.[107]

Johannes Volkelt (1848–1930), Wölfflin's teacher, praised Lotze and Robert Vischer for viewing objects as containing movement and force.

[105] Of course, Riegl's *Kunstwollen* was not merely a product of animism but was also influenced by many intellectual trends. Here, I only aim to reveal the concepts that might have been shared among art historians of that time.

[106] Robert Vischer, 'On the Optical Sense of Form: A Contribution to Aesthetics', p. 109.

[107] Lionello Venturi, *History of Art Criticism*, p. 206.

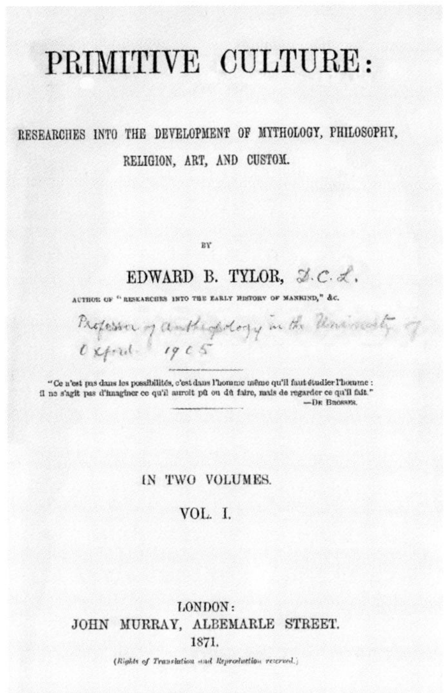

PRIMITIVE CULTURE:

RESEARCHES INTO THE DEVELOPMENT OF MYTHOLOGY, PHILOSOPHY, RELIGION, ART, AND CUSTOM.

BY

EDWARD B. TYLOR, D.C.L.

AUTHOR OF "RESEARCHES INTO THE EARLY HISTORY OF MANKIND," &c.

Professor of Anthropology in the University of Oxford. 1905

"Ce n'est pas dans les possibilités, c'est dans l'homme même qu'il faut étudier l'homme : il ne s'agit pas d'imaginer ce qu'il auroit pû ou dû faire, mais de regarder ce qu'il fait."
—De Brosses.

IN TWO VOLUMES.

VOL. I.

LONDON:
JOHN MURRAY, ALBEMARLE STREET.
1871.

(Rights of Translation and Reproduction reserved.)

Figure 22. *Primitive Culture, Volume I* (1871) by Edward Tylor

He declared that 'symbolism and aesthetic significance only emerge when non-human objectivity becomes anthropomorphised or adopts familiar modes of expression'.[108] Wölfflin expressed similar ideas in his doctoral dissertation: 'Forms become meaningful to us only because we recognize in them the expression of a sentient soul. Instinctively we animate each object. This is a primeval instinct of man.' Once this instinct is lost, art perishes with it. He emphasised that his aim was not to find the appearance of a human being in inorganic nature but, rather, to 'interpret the physical world through the categories that we share with it. We also define the expressive capabilities of these other forms accordingly. They can communicate to us only when we ourselves use their qualities to

[108] Johannes Volkelt, *Der Symbol-Begriff in der neuesten Aesthetik*, Jena: Hermann Dufft, 1876, S. 68.

express.'[109] Guided by this theory of empathy, Wölfflin, naturally, posed the following question with a direct animistic sense: 'How is it possible that architectural forms are able to express an emotion or a mood?' Even before Riegl introduced the concept of will in *Problems of Style*, Wölfflin proposed that 'in everything there is a will that struggles to become form and has to overcome the resistance of a formless matter.'[110]

When we shift our focus to Warburg and his *Kulturwissenschaft*, it seems unnecessary to specifically discuss the concept of animism. One of the main ways in which he diverged from traditional art history lay in his comprehensive approach to cultural phenomena. His research encompassed everything – from fine art to minor arts and even non-art – to trace the creation and evolution of images in the process of civilisation. Wundt also explored animism in his *Völkerpsychologie*. As one of Wundt's readers, Warburg borrowed the idea of a universal anthropology of images from this work; he considered all images to be phenomena arising from various cultures throughout history.[111] We must recognise that, in many cases, animism and the concept of empathy are intertwined. In this regard, the symbolic theory of Friedrich Theodor Vischer had a profound influence on Warburg. Vischer, in a somewhat mystical and ambiguous manner, pointed out that when we perceive the beauty of pure forms or even a particular landscape, we project emotions that originate from ourselves. Thus, he essentially defined architecture as symbolic art, where the spirit of art assigned it the task of rhythmically endowing form with life. This is why we can perceive movement in the appearance of architecture, the rise and fall of lines, and the flow of curves through space, as if 'the ear hears the echoing sounds that reverberate from these movements'. Through this ensemble of symbolic effects, Friedrich Theodor Vischer saw architecture as cultural art expressing 'the whole outer and inner life of nations.'[112]

Although Warburg avoided the art historical approach of studying the

---

109 Heinrich Wölfflin, 'Prolegomena to a Psychology of Architecture', p. 152.

110 Heinrich Wölfflin, 'Prolegomena to a Psychology of Architecture', pp. 149, 159.

111 Georges Didi-Huberman, *The Surviving Image*, p. 24.

112 Friedrich Theodor Vischer, *Aesthetik, oder Wissenschaft des Schönen*, Robert Vischer (Hrg.), Munich: Meyer & Jessen, 1922–1923, quoted from Harry Francis Mallgrave and Eleftherios Ikonomou, 'Introduction', p. 19.

autonomous development of art and was wary of purely formal visual analysis, like many *Kunstwissenschaftlers* of his time, he borrowed concepts extensively from psychology, such as empathy and energy. While he had, undoubtedly, a deep interest in problems of style, he consciously reminded himself not to view art history merely as a history of style. Though benefiting from psychology, Warburg did not adopt the concepts of the eye and the body based on visual perception models. Instead, he transformed Wundt's theory of movement, as accessed through Schmarsow, into the idea of human expression in images preserved in memories. In contrast, art historians like Schmarsow focused on the role of movement in the creative or cognitive processes of the artist or beholder. Premising the psychological creation of artworks, Warburg explored the meaning and history of symbols and images. He also employed psychology to observe the progression of civilisation, maintaining that actions and values were not determined by reason alone but also by the mental structure of rationality, emotion and volition within individuals or within particular epochs.[113]

Psychology brought to the study of art not only various methodological approaches but also, more importantly, an academic framework that fundamentally transformed the earlier Romantic narrative model of art history. From this perspective, for both *Kunstwissenschaft* and *Kulturwissenschaft*, the key to explaining stylistic changes lies in psychology and the relationship between the human body and the world, though they took different directions. We see that the relativism approach originating with Herder found its theoretical counterpart in the psychological turn of art studies. Researchers no longer evaluated artworks based on their level of sophistication; instead, they sought to understand the laws, driving forces or spiritual motives behind cultural phenomena. Moreover, they aimed to develop an art history without names or even without time.

[113] Felix Gilbert, 'From Art History to the History of Civilization: Gombrich's Biography of Aby Warburg', *The Journal of Modern History*, Vol. 44, No. 3 (Sep. 1972), pp. 386–7; G. Bing, 'A. M. Warburg', p. 301.

4. Heredity and Variation

The *Kunstwissenschaft* of the nineteenth century was influenced not only by studies of emotion and empathy in aesthetics and psychology but also by Darwin and the broader biological context underlying his theories, as many recent scholars have thoroughly explored. Therefore, when discussing the intellectual background of *Kunstwissenschaft* and *Kulturwissenschaft*, it is necessary, indeed inevitable, to discuss certain concepts derived from biology. First, *Kunstwissenschaft* relies on the achievements of biology on at least two aspects. One is the classification system originating from the natural sciences, which can be traced back to Carl von Linné (1707–1778)[114] and Georges Cuvier (1769–1832), particularly the latter's famous taxonomy that was developed from paleontology research. The other is the theory of empathy in aesthetics, which, in its reference to physiology and psychology, was to a significant extent built upon research in the field biology.

As mentioned earlier, in exploring the relationship between humans and the world, Schmarsow not only advocated psychological observation but also explicitly drew upon Jako Uexküll's biological research.[115] As Schmarsow's competitor for the art history chair at Leipzig University, Wölfflin not only employed physiological psychology in interpreting architectural forms but also established some connection with biological theory through Friedrich von Hausegger (1837–1899). In the bibliography of his doctoral dissertation, Wölfflin listed two works related to music, noting that they had helped shape some of the fundamental ideas of his thesis. One of these was Hausegger's *Die Musik als Ausdruck* (1885), on which Wölfflin even wrote

[114] However, it is important to note that not all art researchers enthusiastically accepted the classification methods of the natural sciences. For example, Luigi Lanzi (1732–1810) explicitly stated that the classification represented by figures such as Carl von Linné or Joseph Pitton de Tournefort (1656–1708) was inapplicable to the narration of painting history: 'In a complete history it is necessary to distinguish each style from every other; nor do I know any more eligible method than by composing a separate history of each school.' Nevertheless, this indirectly reflects that art historians had long been aware of such classification from the natural sciences and were responding to them. See Luigi Lanzi, 'Lanzi's Preface', in *The History of Painting in Italy*, trans. Thomas Roscoe, London: Henry G. Bohn, York Street, Covent Garden, 1847, pp. 14–15.

[115] '...könnte die Auseinandersetzung des Menschen mit der Welt, in die er geboren wird, von hier aus weiter verfolgt werden, indem wir uns auch dabei die biologischen und psychologischen Beobachtungen der neueren Forschung zunutze machen', August Schmarsow, 'Kunstwissenschaft und Kulturphilosophie mit gemeinsamen Grundbegriffen', S. 231.

marginal notes.[116] Hausegger relied not only on physiological literature but also on Darwin's *The Expression of the Emotions in Man and Animals*. He believed that sound, as a form of expression, had a natural connection to the human body and that emotional responses based on sympathy could only be detected through bodily movements such as facial expressions, gestures and postures. Like Hausegger, Wölfflin believed that the process of empathy was directly related to bodily and emotional responses, which were transferred unconsciously to artworks.[117]

The biological research not only helped shape the physiological-psychological approach to art history but also significantly influenced historical models of artistic evolution. Wölfflin once compared the evolution of architecture to organic biological forms, mistakenly believing that it developed towards increasing perfection. Later, however, he acknowledged that different eras had different patterns of imagination, and while he did recognise a process of development, he also stated, 'it experiences all manner of breaks, constrains, and transformations in the actuality of lived history.... It is safe to say that individual self-contained developments can be distinguished within the one overall development and that the developmental lines of these periods evidence a certain parallelism.... The clarification of the following relationship will also have to be left to more detailed investigations: How much prior visual experience is adopted from the old by a new period style, and how do particular developments merge into a long-term development?'[118] In other words, regarding the causes of development, Wölfflin assumed two possible levels: 'a change in forms of perception is the result of an internal development, a development that, as it were, occurs of its own accord within the perceptual apparatus'; or 'an external impulse that determines the transformation, the changed interest, the altered attitude toward the world'. He believed that both approaches were

[116] A less noticeable fact is that the second advisor for Wölfflin's doctoral dissertation was the musicologist Max Steinitzer (1864–1936). Heinrich Dilly mentioned this in an article discussing the interdisciplinary integration of art history with other disciplines. See Heinrich Dilly, 'Wechselseitige Erhellung – Die Kunstgeschichte und ihre Nachbardisziplinen', in Hans Belting et al (Hrg.), *Kunstgeschichte: Eine Einführung*, Berlin: Dietrich Reimer Verlag, 1988, S.359.

[117] Harry Francis Mallgrave and Eleftherios Ikonomou (eds), *Empathy, Form and Space*, pp. 42–43.

[118] Heinrich Wölfflin, *Principles of Art History*, pp.79–80.

valid: 'each taken solely on its own terms.'[119] From the perspective of biological evolutionary theroy, it is the external stimuli or accidental adaptations that give rise to the diverse styles in art history. Lauren Golden identified a Darwinian-like narrative in Wölfflin's writings. 'New forms are already contained within the old, just as one finds the germ of the new among wilting foliage.' bears a striking resemblance to Darwin's descriptions of tree growth, where he used words such as 'decay', 'fresh buds', 'fossil state', 'branching' and 'ramifications'.[120] Whether or not Wölfflin had directly read *On the Origin of Species* (1859) when he wrote those words, it is clear that his writing paralleled a biological mode of thinking.

When praising Burckhardt's research on late antique art, Riegl used the metaphor of the *Keim* ('germ') to explain how an art historian could 'recognize the seeds and buds of new life even in works of the very late antiquity among signs of death and decay.'[121] Is this merely a coincidence? Both Riegl and Wölfflin not only employed the metaphor of the *Keim* but also used it to suggest a biological model in which a new style emerged from the old one. Wölfflin described artistic development as an interweaving of constant and changing elements – in Darwinian terms, new forms emerging from old styles through inheritance of variation. Whether it is the ornamentation discussed by Riegl in *Stilfragen*, the architecture examined by Wölfflin in his doctoral dissertation, or other representational art forms, they emerge through the transformation of previous styles rather than a direct imitation of natural objects.[122] This is not to say that *Kunstwissenschaftlers* slavishly borrowed Darwin's descriptive language, but, rather, to reveal how they responded to the theory of evolution when dealing with artistic development or models of art history.[123] It has even argued that evolutionary thought provided the conceptual framework for nearly all of Riegl's works.[124]

Wölfflin understood artistic development as follows: 'The development

[119] Heinrich Wölfflin, *Principles of Art History*, p. 308.
[120] Heinrich Wölfflin, *Principles of Art History*, p. 314; Lauren Golden, 'Science, Darwin and Art History', in Lauren Golden (ed.), *Raising the Eyebrow: John Onians and World Art Studies*, Oxford: BAR Publishing, 2001, p. 88.
[121] Alois Riegl, *Late Roman Art Industry*, p. 7.
[122] Alois Riegl, *Stilfragen*, S.5-19; Heinrich Wölfflin, *Principles of Art History*, p. 309.
[123] Matthew Rampley, *The Seductions of Darwin*, p. 140.
[124] Marsha Morton, "Art's 'Contest with Nature'", p. 58.

will be quicker in one case and slower in another. It may happen that a development gets underway and is then broken off, only to be picked up again later on; or a conservative tendency might fork off and run parallel to a progressive tendency, whereby its style takes on a particularly expressive character on account of the contrast.'[125] Darwin described human evolution as proceeding 'by slow and interrupted steps, from a lowly condition to the highest standard lower to the highest standard' across various periods, occasionally reverting to 'some of the Characters of an early Progenitor'.[126] Similarly, Riegl believed that artistic development, spanning thousands of years, was a process of evolution and was characterised by 'spurts of progress mixed with moments of recoil' and 'archaic survival'.[127] Darwin frequently mentioned the reappearance or reversion of certain species' characteristics that had been originally possessed by their ancestors and which had remained dormant in successive generations.[128] After generations of selection and variation, traits of an earlier species might appear in new ones. Wölfflin, adopting a periodic view, found oppositions similar to those between the classical and the Baroque in both modern and ancient times, while Riegl, likewise, identified 'baroque' qualities in Roman ruins.[129] It is *Kunstwollen* that determines which artistic variations are adapted to form a new style, while others remain dormant until a future *Kunstwollen* awakens them.[130] Of course, Riegl and Wölfflin are just the most renowned scholars in *Kunstwissenschaft*, but many other nineteenth-century art historians were

[125] Heinrich Wölfflin, *Principles of Art History*, p. 312.

[126] Charles Darwin, *The Descent of Man and Selection in Relation to Sex*, New York: D. Appleton and Company, 1871, p. 177; Charles Darwin, *The Origin of Species and The Descent of Man*, New York: The Modern Library, n.d., p. 117.

[127] Alois Riegl, *Historical Grammar of the Visual Arts*, p. 251; Alois Riegl, 'Late Roman or Oriental?', trans. Peter Wortsman, in Gert Schiff (ed.), *German Essays on Art History*, p. 177; Alois Riegl, *Late Roman Art Industry*, p. 17.

[128] Charles Darwin, *The Descent of Man and Selection in Relation to Sex*, p. 179. 'When a character which has been lost in a breed, reappears after a great number of generations, the most probable hypothesis is, not that one individual suddenly takes after an ancestor removed by some hundred generations, but that in each successive generation the character in question has been lying latent, and at last under unknown favorable conditions, is developed.' Charles Darwin, *On the Origin of Species by Means of Natural Selection*, New York: Appleton, 1896, p. 196.

[129] Heinrich Wölfflin, *Principles of Art History*, p. 310; Margaret Olin, *Forms of Representation in Alois Riegl's Theory of Art*, p. 35.

[130] Marsha Morton, 'Art's "Contest with Nature"', p. 59.

also influenced by the theory of evolution, for example, Semper, Wickhoff and Dvořák. Additionally, anthropologists such as Alfred Haddon (1855–1940) and Henry Balfour (1863–1939) described the history of artistic ornamentation from an evolutionary perspective, attempting to establish genealogies of the development of artefacts.[131]

Within the *Kulturwissenschaft* framework, Warburg innovatively attempted to establish a fluid historical model of images under a seemingly evolutionary framework. Compared to his colleagues in art history, he more explicitly emphasised the role of the concept of survivals in the evolution of images. For example, for fifteenth-century Italians, antiquity became their model, and Warburg thereby identified the significance of the forces that determined style.[132] The model of development in the history of images that he sought to establish was, in his own words, 'an evolutionary theory'.[133] Even in forms that have been transmitted to the present and are already in decline, various postures from classical art could still evoke corresponding emotional responses. Warburg viewed these poses or *Pathosformeln* as diminished traces of a waning past. The survivals from antiquity were continually adapted and transformed into contemporary appearances, a process of image adaptation that Warburg termed *Auseinandersetzung*.[134]

Warburg's concept of *Nachleben* was not exclusive to him, as many scholars of the time were using this term. Didi-Huberman observed that Warburg's friend Schlosser used the English word 'survival' rather than its German equivalent in his writings, as the term had originated in Anglo-Saxon anthropology, specifically from Edward Tylor's *Primitive Culture*.[135] Although Didi-Huberman himself acknowledged that this book could not be considered a direct theoretical source for Warburg, its discussions on the phenomenon of survivals in culture remain an indispensable reference when studying Warburg's concept of *Kulturwissenschaft*. As an anthropologist, Tylor also referenced Darwin, but he was interested in the 'unfit and inappropriate'

131 Matthew Rampley, *The Seductions of Darwin*, pp. 7–8.
132 Aby Warburg, 'Sandro Botticellis, Geburt der Venus "und, Frühling"', S. 5.
133 Aby Warburg, 'Italienische Kunst und internationale Astrologie im Palazzo Schifanoja zu Ferrara', S. 478.
134 G. Bing, A. M. Warburg, p. 310.
135 Didi-Huberman, *The Surviving Image*, p. 35.

cultural elements, while natural selection focused on 'survival of the fittest'.[136] Gombrich seemed to agree with this view, suggesting that while Tylor was fascinated by residues of a past phase, Warburg was more concerned with 'revival'.[137] Therefore, we witness the intricate interplay between art history, anthropology, the theory of evolution, and biology.

Warburg called on art historians to establish general *Entwicklungs-Kategorien* ('evolutionary categories'). In order to achieve this goal, he turned to anthropology and ideas from psychology and biology.[138] Just as anthropology lacked a temporal dimension, Warburg ultimately developed a historical model that disregarded chronological order. At the 1912 Comité International d'Histoire de l'Art, he advocated for art historians to cross the 'borders' of disciplines, and when he recalled his journey to New Mexico nearly thirty years earlier in the form of a lecture, he had in fact already realized his long-held aspiration: building a bridge between the primitive culture of Indigenous people, devoid of historical consciousness, and the classical tradition of Europe.

5. Further Reflections

The lecture on *Schlangenritual* provides us with a key insight into Warburg's intellectual world and prompts reflection on the constellation of knowledge formed at the intersection of *Kunstwissenschaft*, *Kulturwissenschaft*, and other disciplines. Although Warburg conducted his research under *Kulturwissenschaft*, he was committed to the issues of art history throughout his life. Even his final and most elusive project, *Bilderatlas Mnemosyne*, reveals his efforts to reshape problems of style.[139] In one note, he wrote the phrase 'kunstgeschichtliche Kulturwissenschaft' ('art historical cultural studies').[140] Warburg was dissatisfied with solely aesthetic approaches to art history and openly opposed 'the autonomy of artistic developments and the unconnected spontaneity of artistic creation, or against the overrating of

[136] *Ibid.*, p. 35.

[137] E.H. Gombrich, *Aby Warburg*, p. 16.

[138] Aby Warburg, 'Italienische Kunst und internationale Astrologie im Palazzo Schifanoja zu Ferrara', S. 478.

[139] Didi-Huberman, *The Surviving Image*, p. 24.

[140] WIA III.113.6; The draft prepared for a seminar, from November 1927 to December 1928, 118: 'Über die Methode einer kunstgeschichtlichen Kulturwisse – A Stratigraphy of the Warburg Institute Photographic Collection's System' *Visual Resources*, p. 216.

purely formal criteria for the understanding of works of art'.[141] In a letter filled with admiration addressed to Franz Boas, Warburg sincerely explained the academic focus of his library: first, an emphasis on the internal psychological problems, and, secondly, the historical context of images.[142] Warburg and his contemporary *Kunstwissenschaftlers* shared a keen interest in psychology with physiological characteristics. However, while his colleagues regarded the historical context associated with images as merely a non-deterministic factor leading to the stylistic diversity of art, Warburg believed that style and images could never be discussed apart from their historical context. They all turned to anthropology, focusing on the intellectual consistency of humanity, seeking certain stereotypes that could transcend geographical limitations in primitive cultures and so-called minor arts. Furthermore, taxonomy in biology and the theory of evolution provided art history with a classification system for styles and a temporal developmental model, fundamentally transforming the narrative strategies of traditional art history.

Art historians drew on concepts from disciplines such as natural sciences, the theory of evolution, psychology, theory of empathy and anthropology to establish the foundations of their methodologies. At the same time, however, they revealed an ambition to assert the independence of their own discipline. Of course, many other important ideas inspired the development of *Kunstwissenschaft* and *Kulturwissenschaft*, but it is neither necessary nor possible to trace all of them in this book. My initial aim was to highlight the fundamental academic background in which modern art history was shaped through mutual inspiration with various intellectual fields of the nineteenth century, offering another perspective to the historiographical context that has primarily been constructed from within art history itself. Although Warburg chose a different name and even a different path for his work, he shared many of the same intellectual sources with scholars conducting research in the name of *Kunstwissenschaft*. The knowledge frameworks of *Kulturwissenschaft* and

[141] G. Bing, 'A. M. Warburg', p. 301; Aby Warburg, 'Memories of a Journey Through the Pueblo Region', in Philippe-Alain Michaud, *Aby Warburg and the Image in Motion*, p. 301.

[142] Benedetta Cestelli Guidi, 'Aby Warburg and Franz Boas: Two Letters from the Warburg Archive: The Correspondence Between Franz Boas and Aby Warburg (1924-1925)', p. 225.

Kunstwissenschaft are not strictly separate; rather, they often overlap and intertwine. In his autobiography, Karl Popper recalled a discussion with his father about the meaning of words, from which he learnt 'the principle of never arguing about words and their meanings, because such arguments are specious and insignificant.'[143]

[143] Karl Popper, *Unended Quest: An Intellectual Autobiography*, Taylor and Francis e-Library, 2005, pp. 13–14.

BIBLIOGRAPHY

Sources

Augustine, *Confessions*, trans. William Watts, London: William Heinemann, 1912.

Bastian, Adolf, 'Review of Völkerkunde by Oscar Peschel', *Zeitschrift für Ethnologie*, 6, 1874.

—'The Psychic Unity of Mankind and Some Elementary Symbols', in *Adolf Bastian and the Psychic Unity of Mankind: The Foundations of Anthropology in Nineteenth Century Germany*, Münster: LIT Verlag, 2005, pp. 179–185.

Boas, Franz, *Primitive Art*, Oslo: H. Aschehoug & Company, 1927.

Cassirer, Ernst, *Zur Logik der Kulturwissenschaften: Fünf Studien*, Göteborg: Elanders boktryckeri aktiebolag, 1942.

— *The Myth of the State*, New Haven and London: Yale University Press, 1946.

— *The Logic of the Humanities*, New Haven: Yale University Press, 1961.

— *The Logic of the Cultural Sciences*, New Haven: Yale University Press, 2000.

Coellen, Ludwig, Über die *Methode der Kunstgeschichte: eine geschichtsphilosophische untersuchung*, Darmstadt: Arkadenverlag, 1924.

Darwin, Charles, *The Descent of Man and Selection in Relation to Sex*, New York: D. Appleton and Company, 1871.

— *On The Origin of Species by Means of Natural Selection*, New York: Appleton, 1896.

— *The Origin of Species and The Descent of Man, New York: The Modern Library,* n.d.

Hume, David, *An Enquiry Concerning Human Understanding*, Oxford: Oxford University Press, 2007, p. 60.

Dessoir, Max, *Geschichte der neueren deutschen Psychologie*, Berlin: Verlag von Carl Dunker, 1902.

—*Outlines of the History of Psychology*, trans. Donald Fisher, New York: The Macmillian Company, 1912.

Dilthey, Wilhelm, 'The Dream', in *Wilhelm Dilthey's Philosophy of History*, New York: Columbia University Press, 1955, pp. 103–109.

—'Preface', in *Selected Works: Introduction to the Human Sciences*, trans. Michael Neville, Princeton: Princeton University Press, Vol. 1, 1989, pp. 47–52.

Dvořák, Max, *Römische Kunst*, Berlin: Meyer & Jessen, 1912.

Grosse, Ernst, *Die Anfänge der Kunst*, Freiburg: J. C. B. Mohr, 1894.

— *The Beginnings of Art*, New York: D. Appleton and Company, 1897.

Hanslick, Eduard, *Vom Musikalisch-Schönen*, Leipzig: Rudolph Weigel, 1854.

— *The Beautiful in Music: A Contribution to the Revisal of Musical Aesthetics*, trans. Gustav Cohen, London: Novello, 1891.

Hartel, Wilhelm Ritter von und Wickhoff, Franz, *Die Wiener Genesis*, Wien: F. Tempsky, *Jahrbuch der Kunsthistorischen Sammlungen des Allerhöchsten Kaiserhauses*, 15, 16 (1895).

Helmholtz, Hermann von, *Die Thatsachen in der Wahrnehmung: Rede gehalten zur Stiftungfeier der Friedrich-Wilhelms-Universität zu Berlin am 3. August 1878*, Berlin: A. Hirschwald, 1879.—*Helmholtz's Treatise on Physiological Optics*, trans. J.P.C. Southall, New York: Dover Publications, 1962.

Herder, Gottfried, 'Kalligone', in *Herders sämtliche Werke*, Berlin: Weidmannsche Buchhandlung, 1880.

Hildebrand, Adolf von, *Das Problem der Form in der bildenden Kunst*, Strassburg: Heitz, 1893.

—*The Problem of Form in Painting and Sculpture*, trans. Max Meyer and Robert Morris Ogden, New York: G. E. Stechert & Co., 1907.

Hirn, Yrjö, *The Origins of Art: A Psychological & Sociological Inquiry*, London: Macmillan & Co., 1900.

Husserl, Edmund, 'Die Philosophie in der Krisis der europäischen Menschheit', in *Die Krisis der europäischen Wissenschaften und die transzendentale Phänomenologie: Eine Einleitung in die phänomenologische Philosophie*, The Hague: Martinus Nijhoff, 1954.

—'Philosophy and the Crisis of European Humanity', in *The Crisis of European Sciences and Transcendental Phenomenology: An Introduction to Phenomenological Philosophy*, trans. David Carr, Evanston: Northwestern University Press, 1970, pp. 269–299.

Ideler, Ludwig, *Handbuch der mathematischen und technischen Chronologie*, Bd. 1, Berlin: August Rücker, 1825.

Luigi Lanzi, "Lanzi's Preface", in *The History of Painting in Italy*, trans. Thomas Roscoe, London: Henry G. Bohn, York Street, Covent Garden, 1847, pp. 11–27.

Newton, Isaac, *The Mathematical Principles of Natural Philosophy*, New York: The Citadel Press, 1964.

Panofsky, Erwin, 'Das Problem des Stils in der bildenden Kunst', *Zeitschrift für Ästhetik und allgemeine Kunstwissenschaft*, 10 (1915), S. 460–67.

—'Der Begriff des Kunstwollens', *Zeitschrift für Ästhetik und allgemeine Kunstwissenschaft*, 14 (1920), S. 321–39.

—'Über das Verhältnis der Kunstgeschichte zur Kunsttheorie', *Zeitschrift für Ästhetik und allgemeine Kunstwissenschaft*, 18 (1925), S. 129–61.

—'Über das Verhältnis der Kunstgeschichte zur Kunsttheorie', in *Aufsätze zu Grundfragen der Kunstwissenschaft*, Berlin: Verlag Bruno Hessling, 1964, S. 49–75.

—'Über das Verhältnis der Kunstgeschichte zur Kunsttheorie', in *Deutschsprachige Aufsätze*, Berlin: Akademie Verlag, 1998, S. 1019–34.

—'Reflections on Historical Time', trans. Johanna Bauman, *Critical Inquiry*, Vol. 30, No. 4 (2004), pp. 691–701.

—'On the Relationship of Art History and Art Theory: Towards the Possibility of a Fundamental System of Concepts for a Science of Art', trans. Katharina Lorenz and Jaś Elsner, *Critical Inquiry*, Vol. 35, No. 1 (Autumn 2008), pp. 43–71.

Riegl, Alois, 'Die mittelalterliche Kalenderillustration', *Mitteilungen des Instituts für* Österreichische Geschichtsforschung, X, 1889, S. 1-74.

—*Stilfragen: Grundlegungen zu einer Geschichte der Ornamentik*, Berlin: George Siemens, 1893.

—'Kunstgeschichte und Universalgeschichte', in *Festgaben zu Ehren Max Büdinger's von seinen Freuden und Schülern*, Innsbruck: Wagner, 1898.

—*Der moderne Denkmalkultus: sein Wesen und seine Entstehung*, Wien und Leipzig: W. Braumüller, 1903.

—'The Modern Cult of Monuments: Its Character and Its Origin', trans. Kurt W. Forster and Diane Ghirardo, *Oppositions*, 25 (Fall 1982), pp. 21–51.

—'The Modern Cult of Monuments: Its Essence and Its Development', in *Readings in Conservation: Historical and Philosophical Issues in the Conservation of Cultural Heritage*, Los Angeles: Getty Conservation Institute, 1996, pp. 69–83.

—'Naturwerk und Kunstwerk', in *Gesammelte Aufsätze*, Ausburg: Dr. Benno Filser Verlag, 1928.

—*Historische Grammatik der bildenden Künste*, Graz u. Köln: Böhlau Verlag, 1966.

—*Late Roman Art Industry*, trans. Rolf Winkes, Roma: Giorgio Bretschneider Editore, 1985.

—'Late Roman or Oriental?', in *German Essays on Art History*, trans. Peter Wortsman, New York: The Continuum Publishing Company, 1988, pp. 173–190.

—*Historical Grammar of the Visual Arts*, trans. Jacqueline E. Jung, New York: Zone Books, 2004.

Schlosser, Julius von., 'The Vienna School of the History of Art – Review of a Century of Austrian Scholarship in German', translated and edited by Karl Johns, *Journal of Art Historiography*, No.1 (2009), pp. 1–50.

Schmarsow, August, *Grundbegriffe der Kunstwissenschaft: am* Übergang *vom Altertum zum Mittelalter kritisch erörtert und in systematischem Zusammenhange dargestellt*, Leipzig: Teubner, 1905.

—'Kunstwissenschaft und Völkerpsychologie: ein Versuch zur Verständigung', *Zeitschrift für Ästhetik und allgemeine Kunstwissenschaft*, 2 (1907), S. 305–39.

—'Kunstwissenschaft und Kulturphilosophie mit gemeinsamen Grundbegriffen', *Zeitschrift für Ästhetik und allgemeine Kunstwissenschaft*, 13, 1919.

Schnaase, Carl, *Geschichte der bildenden Künste*, Düsseldorf: Verlag von Julius Buddeus, 1843.

—*Problems of Style: Foundations for a History of Ornament*, trans. Evelyn Kain, Princeton and New Jersey: Princeton University Press, 1992.

Schopenhauer, Arthur, *The World as Will and Representation*, Vol. 2, trans. E. f. J. Payne, New York: Dover Publications, Inc., 1969.

Sedlmayr, Hans, 'Zu einer strengen Kunstwissenschaft', Otto Pächt (Hrg.), *Kunstwissenschaftliche Forschungen*, Vol. 1, 1931, S. 7–32.

—'Kunstgeschichte als Kunstgeschichte', in *Kunst und Wahrheit*, Mittenwald: Mäander, 1978.

—'Toward a Rigorous Study of Art', in *The Vienna School Reader: Politics and Art Historical Method in the 1930s*, trans. Mia Fineman, New York: Zone Books, 2000, pp. 133–79.

—'The Quintessence of Riegl's Thought', in *Framing Formalism: Riegl's Work*, London: Routledge, 2001, pp. 11–31.

Semper, Gottfried, *Der Stil in den technischen und tektonischen Künsten oder praktische Ästhetik*, Bd. 2, München: Friedrich Bruckmann's Verlag, 1863.

— *Selected Writings of Hermann von Helmholtz*, Russell Kahl (ed.),Connecticut: Wesleyan University Press, 1971.

—'On the Origin of Some Architectural Styles', *RES: Anthropology and Aesthetics*, Vol. 9 (Spring 1985), pp. 53–67.

—*Style in the Technical and Tectonic Arts; or, Practical Aesthetics*, Los Angeles: the Getty Research Institute, 2004.

Vischer, Friedrich Theodor, 'Kritik meiner Ästhetik', in *Kritische Gänge*, H. 5, Stuttgart: Cotta, 1866, S. 1–156.

Vischer, Robert, Über das optische Formgefühl: ein Beitrag zur Aesthetik, Leipzig: Hermann Credner, 1873.

—'On the Optical Sense of Form: A Contribution to Aesthetics', in *Empathy, Form and Space: Problems in German Aesthetics 1873–1893*, Harry Francis Mallgrave and Eleftherios Ikonomou (eds), Santa Monica: Getty Center for the History of Art and the Humanities, 1994, pp. 89–123.

Volkelt, Johannes, *Der Symbol-Begriff in der neuesten Aesthetik*, Jena: Hermann Dufft, 1876.

Waitz, Theodore, *Introduction to Anthropology*, in *Anthropology of Primitive Peoples*, Vol. 1, London: The Anthropological Society, 1863.

Warburg, Aby, 'Italienische Kunst und internationale Astrologie im Palazzo Schifanoja zu Ferrara', in *Gesammelte Schriften*, Gertrud Bing (Hrg.), Leipzig and Berlin: B. G. Teubner, Bd. 2, 1932, S. 459–481.

—'Sandro Botticellis, Geburt der Venus "und, Frühling"', in *Gesammelte Schriften*, Gertrud Bing (Hrg.), Leipzig and Berlin: B. G. Teubner, Bd. 1, 1932, S. 1–59.

—'A Lecture on Serpent Ritual', *Journal of the Warburg Institute*, Vol. 2 (April 1939), pp. 277–292.

—*Schlangenritual: Ein Reisebericht*, Berlin: Wagenbach, 1988.

—*German Essays on Art History*, trans. Peter Wortsman, New York: The Continuum Publishing Company, 1988, pp. 234–54.

—*Images from the Region of the Pueblo Indians of North America*, trans. Michael P. Steinberg, Ithaca: Cornell University Press, 1995.

—*The Renewal of Pagan Antiquity*, trans. David Britt, Los Angeles: The Getty Research Institute, 1999, pp. 563–92.

—'Die Richtungen der Kunstgeschichte. An Adolph Goldschmidt', in *Werke in einem Band*, Berlin: Suhrkamp Verlage, 2010, S. 672–679.

—'Vom Arsenal zum Laboratorium', in *Werke in einem Band*, Berlin: Suhrkamp Verlage, 2010, S. 683–694.

Wickhoff, Franz, *Die Wiener Genesis*, Wien: F. Tempsky, 1895.

—'Ueber die historische Einheitlichkeit der gesamten Kunstentwicklung', in *Festgaben zu Ehren Max Büdinger's von seinen Freuden und Schülern*, Innsbruck: Wagner, 1898, S. 459–469.

—*Aesthetik, oder Wissenschaft des Schönen*, Munich: Meyer & Jessen, 1922-1923.

—*Roman Art: Some of Its Principles and Their Application to Early Christian Painting*, trans. Mrs. S. Arthur Strong, London: W. Heinemann; New York: Macmillan, 1900.

Wind, Edgar, Ästhetischer *und kunstwissenschaftlicher Gegenstand: ein Beitrag zur Methodologie der Kunstgeschichte*, 1922, Philo Verlag, 2012.

—'Zur Systematik der künstlerischen Probleme', *Zeitschrift für Ästhetik und allgemeine Kunstwissenschaft*, 18 (1925), S. 438–86.

—'Warburg's Concept of Kulturwissenschaft and its Meaning for Aesthetics', in *The Eloquence of Symbols: Studies in Humanist Art*, Oxford: Clarendon Press, 1983, pp. 21–35.

Wölfflin, Heinrich, *Prolegomena zu einer Psychologie der Architektur*, München: Kgl. Hof- & Universitäts-Buchdruckerei von Dr. C. Wolf & Sohn, 1886.

—'Prolegomena to a Psychology of Architecture', in *Empathy, Form and Space: Problems in German Aesthetics 1873–1893*, Harry Francis Mallgrave and Eleftherios Ikonomou (eds), Santa Monica: Getty Center for the History of Art and the Humanities, 1994.

—'Das Problem des Stils in der bildenden Kunst', in *Sitzungsberichte der königlich preußischen Akademie der Wissenschaften*, 1912.

—*Kunstgeschichtliche Grundbegriffe: das Problem der Stilentwicklung in der neueren Kunst*, München: F. Bruckmann A.-G., 1915.

—*Principles of Art History: The Problem of the Development of Style in Early Modern Art*, trans. Jonathan Blower, Los Angeles: The Getty Research Institute, 2015.

—*Die Klassische Kunst: Eine Einführung in die italienische Renaissance*, München: F. Bruckmann A.-G. 1924.

—*Renaissance and Baroque*, trans. Kathrin Simon, Ithaca, New York: Cornell University Press, 1964.

Wood, Christopher S. (ed.), *The Vienna School Reader: Politics and Art Historical Method in the 1930s*, New York: Zone Books, 2000.

—*A History of Art History*, Princeton and Oxford: Princeton University Press, 2019.

Zimmerman, Andrew, *Anthropology and the Place of Knowledge in Imperial Berlin*, San Diego: University of California, 1998.

—*Anthropology and Antihumanism in Imperial Germany*, Chicago and London: The University of Chicago Press, 2001.

Studies

Antoni, Carlo, *Dallo storicismo alla sociologia*, Firenze: Sansoni, 1940.

Arens, Katherine, *Structures of Knowing: Psychologies of the Nineteenth Century*, Dordrecht, Boston, London: Kluwer Academic Publishers, 1989.

Bakoš, Ján, 'The Vienna School's Views of the Structure of the Art Historical Process', in *Wien und die Entwicklung der kunsthistorischen Methode*, Wien, Köln, Graz: Hermann Böhlaus Nachfolger, 1984, pp. 117–122.

Białostocki, Jan, 'Erwin Panofsky (1892–1968): Thinker, Historian, Human Being', *Simiolus*, Vol. 4, No. 2 (1970), pp. 68–89.

Bing, G., 'A. M. Warburg', *Journal of the Warburg and Courtauld Institutes*, Vol. 28 (1965), pp. 299–313.

Bock, Henning, *Adolf von Hildebrand: Gesammelte Schriften zur Kunst*, Cologne: Westdeutscher Verlag, 1969, S. 17–33.

Burke, Peter, 'History and Anthropology in 1900', in *Photographs at the Frontier: Aby Warburg in America 1895-1896*, Benedetta Cestelli Guidi and Nicholas Mann (eds),London: The Warburg Institute, 1998, pp. 20–27.

Collingwood, R.G., *The Idea of History*, Oxford: Clarendon Press, 1946.

Didi-Huberman, Georges, *The Surviving Image: Phantoms of Time and Time of Phantoms. Aby Warburg's History of Art*, trans. Harvey L. Mendelsohn, Pennsylvania: The Pennsylvania State University Press, 2017.

Heinrich Dilly, 'Wechselseitige Erhellung – Die Kunstgeschichte und ihre Nachbardisziplinen', in Hans Belting et al (Hrg.), *Kunstgeschichte: Eine Einführung*, Berlin: Dietrich Reimer Verlag, 1988, S.351–365.

Elsner, Jas, *Art History, The Global Turn and the Possibilities of Comparativism* (《全球转向下的艺术史：从欧洲中心主义到比较主义》), trans. Hu Moran (胡默然) et al., Shanghai: Shanghai People's Publishing House, 2022.

Fan, Baiding, "Some Theoretical Sources of Iconology Studies" (《〈图像学研究〉的一些理论来源》), in *World 3: Open Iconology* (《世界3：开放的图像学》), Beijing: China National Photographic Art Publishing House, 2017, pp. 150–169.

Ferretti, Silvia, *Cassirer, Panofsky, and Warburg: Symbol, Art and History*, New Haven and London: Yale University Press, 1989.

Flach, Sabine, 'Communicating Vessels: On the Development of a Theory of Representation in Darwin and Warburg', in *Darwin and Theories of Aesthetics and Cultural History*, Barbar Larson and Sabine Flach (eds), Surrey: Ashgate, 2013, pp. 109–124.

Fleckner, Uwe (Hrg.), *Aby Warburg, Bilder aus dem Gebiet der Pueblo-Indianer in Nord-Amerika: Vorträge und Fotografien*, Band III.2 in *Gesammelte Schriften*, Berlin: de Gruyter, 2018.

Forster, Kurt W., 'Monument/Memory and the Mortality of Architecture', in *Oppositions Reader: Selected Essays 1973–1984*, New York: Princeton Architectural Press, 1998, pp. 18–35.

Freedberg, David, 'Pathos a Oraibi: Ciò che Warburg non vide', in *Lo Sguardo di Giano. Aby Warburg fra tempo e memoria*, Turin: Nino Aragno, 2004, pp. 569–611.

—'Warburg's Mask: A Study in Idolatry', in *Anthropologies of Art*, Williamstown, Massachusetts: Sterling and Francine Clark Art Institute, 2005, pp. 3–25.

Gantner, Joseph (Hrg.), *Heinrich Wölfflin, 1864–1945: Autobiographie, Tagebücher und Briefe*, Basel: Benno Schwabe, 1982.

Gilbert, Felix, 'From Art History to the History of Civilization: Gombrich's Biography of Aby Warburg', *The Journal of Modern History*, Vol. 44, No. 3, (1972), pp. 381–391.

Glockner, Hermann, 'Robert Vischer und die Krisis der Geisteswissenschaften imletzten Drittel des neunzehnten Jahrhunderts', *Logos: Internationale Zeitschrift für Philosophie der Kultur*, 15 (1926), S. 47–102

Golden, Lauren, 'Science, Darwin and Art History', in *Raising the Eyebrow: John Onians and World Art Studies*, Oxford: BAR Publishing, 2001, 79–90.

Gombrich, E.H., 'Kunstwissenschaft', in *Atlantisbuch der Kunst,* Zürich: Atlantis – Verlag, 1952, S. 653–664.

—'In Search of Cultural History', *Ideals and Idols: Essays on Values in History and in Art*, Oxford: Phaidon, 1979, pp. 24–59.

—*Aby Warburg: An Intellectual Biography*, Oxford: Phaidon, 1986.

Gubser, Michael, *Time's Visible Surface: Alois Riegl and the Discourse on History and Temporality in Fin-de-Siècle Vienna*, Detroit: Wayne State University Press, 2006.

Guidi, Benedetta Cestelli, and Mann, Nicholas (eds), *Photographs at the Frontier: Aby Warburg in America 1895–1896*, London: The Warburg Institute, 1998.

Guidi, Benedetta Cestelli, 'Aby Warburg and Franz Boas: Two Letters from the Warburg Archive', *RES: Anthropology and Aesthetics*, Vol. 52 (2007), pp. 221–230.

Halbertsma, Marlite, 'The Many Beginnings and the One End of World Art History in Germany 1900-1933', in *World Art Studies: Exploring Concepts and Approaches*, Amsterdam: Valiz, 2008, pp. 91–105.

Hart, Joan, 'Some Reflections on Wölfflin and the Vienna School', in *Wien und die Entwicklung der Kunsthistorischen Methode*, Vienna: Böhlau, 1984, pp. 53–64.

Hawking, Stephen, *A Brief History of Time*, New York: Bantam Books, 1988.

Holly, Michael Ann, *Panofsky and the Foundations of Art History*, Ithaca and London: Cornell University Press, 1984.

Iggers, Georg, *The German Conception of History: The National Tradition of Historical Thought from Herder to the Present*, Middletown, Connecticut: Wesleyan University Press, 1983.

Imbert, Claude, 'Aby Warburg, Between Kant and Boas: From Aesthetics to the Anthropology of Images', *Qui Parle*, Vol. 16, No. 1 (2006), pp. 1–45.

Johnston, William M., *The Austrian Mind: An Intellectual and Social History 1848–1938*, Berkeley, Los Angeles, London: University of California Press, 1972.

Kany, Roland, *Mnemosyne als Programm. Geschichte, Erinnerung und die Andacht zum Unbedeutenden im Werk von Usener, Warburg und Benjamin*, Tübingen: Niemeyer, 1987.

Kaschnitz-Weinberg, Guido, 'Alois Riegl. Spätrömische Kunstindustrie. Rezension', *Gnomon*, 5, Bd., H. 4/5, 1929.

—'Review of Alois Riegl, *Die Spätrömische Kunstindustrie*, 1927', trans. Martin Schwarz, *Art History*, 39 (1), 2016, pp. 85–97.

Levy, Evonne, 'Wölfflin's *Principles of Art History* (1915–2015): A Prolegomenon for Its Second Century', in *Principles of Art History*, Los Angeles: The Getty Research Institute, 2015, pp. 1–46.

Mallgrave, Harry Francis and Ikonomou, Eleftherios (eds), *Empathy, Form and Space: Problems in German Aesthetics 1873–1893*, Santa Monica: Getty Center for the History of Art and the Humanities, 1994, pp. 1–85.

Mandelbaum, Maurice, *History, Man and Reason: A Study in Nineteenth-Century Thought*, Baltimore: Johns Hopkins University Press, 1971.

Mazzucco, Katia, 'Images on the Move: Some Notes on the Bibliothek Warburg Bildersammlung (Hamburg) and the Warburg Institute Photographic Collection (London)', *Art Libraries*, Vol. 38, No. 4 (2013), pp. 16–24.

—'(Photographic) Subject-matter: Fritz Saxl Indexing Mnemosyne

—A Stratigraphy of the Warburg Institute Photographic Collection's System', *Visual Resources*, 2014, pp. 201–221.

Meyerhoff, Hans (ed.), *The Philosophy of History in Our Time*, Garden City, New York: Doubleday Anchor Books, 1959.

Michaud, Philippe-Alain, *Aby Warburg and the Image in Motion*, trans. Sophie Haukes, New York: Zone Books, 2004.

Morton, Marsha, 'Art's "Contest with Nature": Darwin, Haeckel, and the Scientific Art History of Alois Riegl', in *Darwin and Theories of Aesthetics and Cultural History*, Surrey: Ashgate, 2013, pp. 53–68.

Moxey, Keith, *Visual Time: The Image in History*, Durham and London: Duke University Press, 2013.

Naber, Claudia, 'Pompeji in Neu-Mexico: Aby Warburgs amerikanische Reise', *Freibeuter*, 38 (1988), S. 88–97.

Neher, Allister, '"The Concept of Kunstwollen", Neo-Kantianism, and Erwin Panofsky's Early Art Theoretical Essays', *Word & Image*, Vol. 20, No. 1 (2004), p. 41–51.

Olin, Margaret, *Forms of Representation in Alois Riegl's Theory of Art*, Pennsylvania: The Pennsylvania State University Press, 1992.

Pächt, Otto, 'Art Historians and Art Critics-vi: Alois Riegl', *The Burlington Magazine*, Vol. 105, No. 722 (1963), 188–193.

—*The Practice of Art History: Reflections on Method*, trans. David Britt, London: Harvey Miller Publishers, 1999.

—'The End of the Image Theory', in *The Vienna School Reader: Politics and Art Historical Method in the 1930s*, New York: Zone Books, 2000, pp. 181–194.

Papapetros, Spyros, 'World Ornament: The Legacy of Gottfried Semper's 1856 Lecture on Adornment', *RES: Anthropology and Aesthetics*, No. 57/58 (2010), pp. 309–329.

Pfisterer, Ulrich (Hrg.), 'Origins and Principles of World Art History: 1900 (and 2000)', in *World Art Studies: Exploring Concepts and Approaches*, Amsterdam: Valiz, 2008, pp. 69–89.

—*Metzler Lexikon Kunstwissenschaft: Ideen, Methoden, Begriffe*, 2., erweiterte und aktualisierte Auflage, Stuttgart, Weimar: Verlag J. B. Metzler, 2011.

Pinotti, Andrea, 'Body-Building: August Schmarsow's *Kunstwissenschaft* Between Psychophysiology and Phenomenology', in *German Art History and Scientific Thought: Beyond Formalism*, Surrey: Ashgate, 2012, pp. 13–31.

Podro, Michael, *The Critical Historians of Art*, New Haven and London: Yale University Press, 1982.

Popper, Karl, *Unended Quest: An Intellectual Autobiography*, Taylor and Francis e-Library, 2005.

Prange, Regine, *Die Geburt der Kunstgeschichte: Philosophische Ästhetik und empirische Wissenschaft*, Köln: Deubner Verlag für Kunst, Theorie & Praxis, 2004.

Rampley, Matthew, 'Iconology of the Interval: Aby Warburg's Legacy', *Word & Image*, Vol. 17, No. 4 (2001), pp. 203–324.

—*The Seductions of Darwin: Art, Evolution, Neuroscience*, University Park: Penn State University Press, 2017.

Sassi, Maria Michela, 'Dalla Scienza delle Religioni di Usener ad Aby Warburg', in *Aspetti di Hermann Usener Filologo della Religione*, Pisa: Giardini, 1982, pp. 65–91.

Saxl, Fritz, 'Warburg's Visit to New Mexico', in *Lectures*, London: Warburg Institute, 1957, pp. 325–330.

Schapiro, Meyer, 'The New Viennese School', *Art Bulletin*, Vol. 18, No. 2 (1936), pp. 258–266.

Schwarz, Martin and Elsner, Jaś, 'The Genesis of *Struktur*: Kaschnitz-Weinberg's Review of Riegl and the New Viennese School', *Art History*, 39 (1), 2016, pp. 71–83.

Settis, Salvatore, 'Kunstgeschichte als vergleichende Kulturwissenschaft: Aby Warburg, die Pueblo-Indianer und das Nachleben der Antike', *Künstlerischer*

Austausch/Artistic Exchange, Akten des XXVIII. *Internationalen Kongresses für Kunstgeschichte Berlin 1992*, Bd. 1, Berlin: Akademie Verlag, 1993, S. 139–158.

Stanford, Michael, *A Companion to the Study of History*, Oxford UK & Cambridge USA: Blackwell, 1994.

Stimilli, Davide, 'Aby Warburg in America again', *RES: Anthropology and Aesthetics*, No. 48 (2005), pp. 193–206

Paul Taylor, "Henri Frankfort, Aby Warburg and 'Mythopoeic Thought'", *Journal of Art Historiography*, No. 5 (2011), p. 1–16.

Venturi, Lionello, *History of Art Criticism*, trans. Charles Marriott, New York: E. P. Dutton & Company, Co., Inc., 1964.

White, Hayden, 'On History and Historicism', in *From History to Sociology: The Transition in German Historical Thinking*, trans. Hayden White, London: Merlin Press, 1962, pp. xv-xviii.

Wiesing, Lambert, *Die Sichtbarkeit des Bildes: Geschichte und Perspektiven der formalen Ästhetik*, Rowohlt Taschenbuch Verlag, 1997.

—*The Visibility of the Image: History and Perspectives of Formal Aesthetics*, trans. Nancy Ann Roth, New York: Bloomsbury Academic, 2016.

Winkes, Rolf, 'Foreword', in Alois Riegl, *Late Roman Art Industry*, trans. Rolf Winkes, Roma: Giorgio Bretschneider Editore, 1985.

INDEX